Game Cookery

Also by Patricia Lousada

American Sampler

A Book of Chocolate

A Book of Sweets

The Chocolate Lover's Cookbook

Cooking with Herbs

Easy to Entertain

Food for Presents

The Great American Bake-In

Pasta Italian Style

Game Cookery

PATRICIA LOUSADA

JOHN MURRAY

For Anthony

First published 1989
by John Murray (Publishers) Ltd
50 Albemarle Street, London W1X 4BD

British Library Cataloguing in Publication Data

Lousada, Patricia
Game cookery.
1. Food: Game dishes — Recipes
I. Title
641.6'91

ISBN 0-7195-4602-8

Illustrations by Dorothy Moir

Typeset by Colset Private Limited
Printed and bound in Great Britain
by Butler & Tanner Ltd, Frome and London

Contents

Acknowledgements

APART from my incredible Mother who is still cooking delicious food daily for friends and family at the age of eighty-nine I owe a great debt to Julia Child and Marcella Hazan. Both authors have opened my eyes to the possibilities of cooking and have played a large role in raising the standards and interest in food in the States. Like so many people in this country I have learned and been inspired by first Elizabeth David and later Jane Grigson, whose writing and recipes continue to be a source of pleasure and information. I am particularly grateful to Jane Grigson for her never-ending generosity over advice and recipes. Sam Clark, a young chef, now at the River Café in London, was a great help and a delightful companion over some of the testing for this book. I would like to thank Jane Mann for her help with research. I am very grateful to Caroline Hobhouse who not only has been an encouraging editor but has also contributed a recipe to the book. I am also grateful to the authors of those recipes from which I have adapted some of mine.

Acknowledgements are found in the text as well as in the bibliography. My thanks to Henrietta Green, the publisher of *British Food Finds*, for her expertise on all aspects of farmed game. The Game Conservancy has been very helpful and patient with my numerous phone calls for information. It is hopeful for the future of game that they are so active and influential over conservation.

Introduction

HUNTING in all its forms has always been a passion of mankind. Tolstoy describes the thrill of departure in the early morning for duck-shooting and the impatience of the dog. Izaac Walton writes of the joys of fishing and Siegfried Sassoon of the lure of fox-hunting. Many cave paintings and Mogul minatures, Renaissance paintings and eighteenth-century British pictures record hunting scenes.

Apart from the excitement of the find and the skill required, the justification of the kill has either been protection of one's neighbours in the case of the Bengal tiger or one's poultry in the case of the fox or for the provision of food. As game became prized as a delicacy it was the landowning upper classes that sought to ensure a constant supply for themselves. Game preserves and breeding grounds date back as far as the Romans and in England from Saxon times. Hunting has played a part in court life from the Middle Ages to the nineteenth century. The ancient practice of falconry, possibly begun in Arabia around 2000 BC, was the king of hunting sports in every European court until the development of reliable guns in the seventeenth century. The 'guns' in their smart tweeds and the local beaters, looking like figures out of a Brueghel painting, can still be seen today, linking the modern world to a long aristocratic tradition.

With increased affluence and the blurring of social distinctions a wider audience has begun to discover and appreciate game. The ever expanding interest in cooking and a concern for healthier diet has put game on the supermarket shelves. Game, as most know by now, is a lean natural meat, free from growth-promoters, and it is not necessarily a luxury item. Rabbit and hare are very good value, pigeon is a great bargain, and the price of pheasant compares favourably with that of free-range chicken. The rich, clear flavour of game is the biggest selling point. With so many foods watered down by mass-production growing methods, at least the true wild game still has real flavour.

General Advice on Game

Because game is a lean meat it needs to be cooked with care. It is also variable. No two wild birds or animals will have had exactly the same diet or exercise, or be the same age. If you are inexperienced at buying game, search out a good game dealer, (often the fishmonger) someone who can give you the background on the bird or beast you are buying. It is crucial to know young from old in order to choose the best cooking method. The game should also be properly hung so it will be as tender and flavourful as is required. The birds are hung unplucked and undrawn by a cord from their necks, separated from each other, in an airy, cool, dry place free from flies. A time guide is given for each bird in the various introductions of this book.

Roasting

Young birds and the tender joints of animals are at their best simply roasted. A roasting time chart is included and the appropriate recipes will also give roasting times as well as ideas for sauces. Any lean meat will dry out if overcooked, and game is no exception. If you want your bird or roast to be juicy it should not be well done. It does not have to be very rare but it should be kept pink, the exceptions being wild boar and wild rabbit which should be cooked through. The smaller birds are cooked briefly at a high temperature, the larger joints are roasted more slowly at lower temperatures. Browning can take place on top of the stove to colour the skin and shorten the oven time. Another method is to roast the bird and serve only the breasts, which cook first; the rest of the bird can be returned to the oven to cook further, either for second helpings, or to be used for the basis of a quick sauce. The latter is a favourite with chefs and useful for home cooking as well when there isn't time for a more conventional stock. The small wishbone on the front of the breast can easily be removed with a small sharp knife before roasting – this will make for easy carving, and a small amount of stuffing inserted in this breast cavity flavours the meat very effectively. The main cavity can also be stuffed; a herb butter, seasoned petit suisse or other soft cream cheese can be used. It is also vital that all joints and birds should rest before they are carved and served. A low oven, a hot plate with a foil cover, or a hot corner of the stove can serve the purpose. This gives the meat time to relax and the juices the chance to redistribute themselves. Resting time depends on size but should be anywhere from 10–30 minutes.

Marinating

A marinade of wine, olive oil and aromatics helps to tenderize tougher braising meat. It also helps flavour the meat and for this reason is useful with farmed game. Wild rabbit is often soaked for 12 hours or overnight in water with added vinegar – 1 tablespoon vinegar to 1 litre ($1\frac{3}{4}$ pints) of water.

Barding and Larding

Game needs all the help it can get to overcome its natural dryness. Basting helps as does roasting birds breast-side down. The classic convention is to cover or 'bard' them with a thin layer of pork back-fat, and game dealers should provide this, although often it is anything but thin. You are on your own with supermarket game, but it is possible to obtain back fat from some supermarkets by asking for it – chill it well before cutting into very thin slices. Many people use unsmoked streaky bacon for this purpose but the risk here is that the strong bacon flavour will overpower the game. A better solution is to wrap the game in caul fat. This is a thin veil of fat which surrounds the stomach cavity of a pig. It is sold by butchers in a stiff piece and will need to be softened in warm water, stretched out and cut to size before being used. It continually bastes the meat as it cooks. Larding is another technique usually used for a haunch of venison or pheasant breasts. Thin strips of back fat are stitched into the top of the meat with the help of a larding needle. You can also make small slits in the meat and stuff them with lardons or strips of fat using a finger. Sometimes these lardons are seasoned first with a mixture of parsley, garlic and salt.

Aging Birds

The most accurate method for determining the age of gamebirds is the 'bursa test'. All young gamebirds have a blind-ending passage above the vent called the bursa. This becomes much reduced or closes when a bird reaches maturity. By inserting the burnt end of a matchstick (it should be narrow but blunt) into the opening, the age of the bird can be established. The precise details for each species are dealt with in the individual introductions. This information is from *The Complete Book of Game Conservation*, a Game Conservancy publication.

Plucking

Pluck outdoors or in a draught-free room and hold the birds inside a large plastic refuse bag. Pull the feathers off starting at the breast, then move on to the sides, back, legs and wings, pulling against the way they lie. Hold the skin taut and when you come to the quills pull these out in the direction of their growth.

Cleaning

Work on newspaper and start by cutting the skin around the neck close to the head. Ease it back and cut through the vertebrae close to the body, then remove the head with the windpipe and crop. Make a cut near the vent, and with your finger, ease round the bony cavity so the entire gut can be pulled out in one go. Keep the heart, gizzard and liver, being careful not to break the gall sac. If the liver has any yellow or green spots, cut them away. Cut the skin off the gizzard and trim the heart. Save these bits for the sauce or stuffing. Wipe out the cavity and cut away the wishbone for easy carving.

Trussing

It is well worth trussing all game birds, not only to keep them in a neat compact shape, but to help them cook more evenly. Thread a trussing needle with thin string. For small birds such as grouse, partridge and quail make a stitch through the upper part of the wings to secure them to the body then pass the needle in the opposite direction through the thighs. Tie the two ends of the string together. For larger birds, such as pheasant, insert the needle through the wing where it bends, catching the folded back flap of neck skin. Pull the needle out through the other wing. Take another stitch through the lower leg and body, remove the needle and tie the two ends of the string together.

Table of Roasting Times and Shooting Seasons for Gamebirds and Animals

Grouse Oven: 190°C/375°F/gas 5 for 35 minutes. Season: 12 August to 10 December.

Partridge Oven: 220°C/425°F/gas 7 for 30 minutes. Season: 1 September to 1 February.

Pheasant Oven: 190°C/375°F/gas 5 for 45–60 minutes, depending on weight. Season: 1 October to 1 February.

Woodcock Oven: 230°C/450°F/gas 8 for 15–20 minutes. Season: England and Wales; 1 October to 31 January Scotland; 1 September to 31 January.

Common Snipe Oven: 230°C/450°F/gas 8 for 10–15 minutes. Season: 12 August to 31 January.

Mallard Oven: 230°C/450°F/gas 8 for 30 minutes for rare; oven: 190°C/375°F/gas 5 for 60 minutes for pink. Season: inland; 1 September to 31 January; below high water mark; 1 September to 20 February.

Widgeon Oven: 230°C/450°F/gas 8 for 15–25 minutes, according to weight. Season: as for Mallard.

Teal Oven: 230°C/450°F/gas 8 for 10–15 minutes, according to weight. Season: as for Mallard.

Wild Goose Young ones only, oven: 220°C/425°F/gas 7 for 15 minutes; then 160°C/325°F/gas 3 for 60 minutes. Braise older birds. Season: as for Mallard.

Rabbit Saddle only, oven: 220°C/425°F/gas 7 for approximately 25 minutes. Whole rabbit: legs splayed out, oven: 190°C/375°F/gas 5, for approximately 60 minutes. No close season.

Hare Saddle only, oven: 220°C/425°F/gas 7 for approximately 25 minutes Whole hare: legs splayed out, oven: 190°C/375°F/gas 5, for approximately 45 minutes. No close season, but cannot be offered for sale during March to July inclusive.

Venison Lard or bard joints. Oven: 230°C/450°F/gas 8 for 20 minutes per kg for rare, 30 minutes for medium rare. Use a meat thermometer for large joints as length of time will vary. Season: Different for each species and sex and covers most months of the year.

[This chart is based on Game Conservancy recommendations.]

GROUSE

Grouse

THE GLORIOUS TWELFTH starts off the game season and it begins with quite a bang – grouse being the bird with a reputation as the best game bird in the world. The red grouse or Scotch grouse, a native of Scotland, the North of England, and the west of Ireland is the envy of many countries. Over the years there have been attempts to introduce it into France but they have not been successful. Grouse feed on young shoots of heather and berries which no doubt contributes to their fine flavour. The season starts on the 12th of August and ends on the 1st of December. The best birds are those born the same year and eaten before mid-October. Ptarmigan, black game and capercaillie are also members of the grouse family but are fairly rare and not considered to be of much culinary merit. (see appendix)

How long grouse should be hung is a matter of taste, but young birds are delicious fresh and it is only a matter of tenderising the older birds. A few days are enough for young grouse, if at all, and a week for older birds in cool weather.

Young grouse can be identified by their flexible breastbone and pointed wings but this is not infallible. The best means of judging age is by the bursa test (see introduction). In young birds the depth of the bursa will be around 1 cm ($\frac{1}{2}$ inch). In older birds the bursa passage closes.

Young grouse are best roasted in a hot oven, stuffed with no more than a knob of butter or a handful of berries. The birds should be barded, or well basted, and not overcooked as they have a tendency to become dry. Older birds can be dealt with by slow braising or in pâtés or pies (chapter 9).

Grouse connoisseurs savour the subtle differences in grouse shot in Derbyshire from those, say, in Perthshire and, as with vintages of wine, compare one year with another.

A late Victorian encylopaedia of cookery attributes this quote to Alexis Soyer. 'Grouse to be well enjoyed should be eaten in secret, and take my experience as your guide: do not let the bird you eat be raw and bloody but well roasted, and drink with it at intervals a little sweet champagne. Never mind your knife and fork; suck the bones, and dwell upon them. Take plenty of time; that is the true way to enjoy a game bird'.

Grouse à la Crème

serves 4

4 grouse (not barded)
1 tablespoon oil
30 g (1 oz) clarified butter
glass of red wine

300 ml ($\frac{1}{2}$ pint) double cream
salt and freshly ground black
    pepper

Wipe the grouse dry and season inside and out with salt and pepper. Heat the oil and butter until it sizzles in a roasting tin. Place the grouse, breast-side down, in a roasting pan and roast in a preheated oven 230°C/450°F/gas 8 for 25 minutes. Turn them on the other side half way through the cooking time. Remove the birds to a warm dish. Deglaze the pan with the red wine, then add the cream and boil hard until the sauce thickens. Season to taste and serve immediately.

Grouse Soufflé

serves 4

A recipe from Mrs De Salis's excellent book '*Dressed Game and Poultry à La Mode*' (1888).

Take the breasts of two grouse already cooked, pound them in a mortar with two ounces of fresh butter and a very small piece of onion. Pass them through a sieve, add four yolks of eggs, beat the whites to a stiff froth, season with a little salt and dust of cayenne. Place it in a soufflé dish and bake it in a quick oven.

Note: The food processor can replace the mortar and pestle, and the sieving too if you don't mind a slightly grainy texture. Individual (well greased) soufflé dishes will only need about 10 minutes, one larger dish 20 minutes, in an oven preheated to 200°C/400°F/gas 6.

——— •●• ———

Casserole of Grouse

serves 4

2 grouse
unsalted butter
1 carrot, diced
2 stick of celery, diced
2 shallots, finely chopped
1 small turnip, diced
150 ml ($\frac{1}{4}$ pint) red wine

300 ml ($\frac{1}{2}$ pint) game stock
bouquet garni
340 g ($\frac{3}{4}$ lb) mushrooms
250 g (8 oz) small pickling onions
some fresh parsley, finely chopped
salt and freshly ground black
    pepper

Cut the grouse into serving pieces. Heat 25 g (1 oz) of butter in a heavy casserole and sauté the vegetables until they are soft and lightly coloured. Remove them from the pan and add the grouse. Brown the grouse on all sides, add the flour and stir a few minutes so the flour is well distributed and colours slightly. Return the vegetables to the casserole along with the bouquet garni. Pour in the wine and reduce by half then add the stock and some salt and pepper if needed. Place a shat of greaseproof paper on top of the ingredients and cover with a tight fitting lid. Simmer very gently for 25 minutes. Meanwhile simmer the onions in 150 ml ($\frac{1}{4}$ pint) of water and a knob of butter until tender. Sauté the mushrooms in another knob of butter. Serve the grouse with the mushrooms and onions decorated with parsley.

Grilled Grouse

serves 4

4 young grouse
olive oil
dried thyme and savory,
lemon juice

fried bread crumbs
rowan jelly
salt and freshly ground black pepper

Split the birds down the back and flatten. Set them on a tray and sprinkle with olive oil and dried herbs and leave for at least 30 minutes. Preheat the grill to medium-high. Season the grouse and grill them about 10 minutes breast-side down, turn over, brush with more olive oil and grill a further 8 minutes. Squeeze a bit of lemon juice over the birds and serve with fried bread crumbs and rowan jelly.

Note: If your grouse came with the livers and hearts, fry them in a bit of butter. Mash, season, spread on fried bread and serve the grilled grouse on top.

Grilled Grouse Marinated in Berry Purée

Jeremiah Tower established his reputation when he was head chef at Chez Panisse in Berkeley, California. Today he is considered to be one of America's most innovative chefs. This recipe, from his book *New American Classics*, was inspired from a seventeenth-century French cookbook, *Le Cuisinier François*. The recipe uses young pigeon but young grouse works even better. The berry marinade adds crispness and colour to the grilled skin.

serves 4

4 grouse, with livers and hearts
450 g (1 lb) raspberries
120 g (4 oz) unsalted butter
4 tablespoons olive oil
230 g (8 oz) slab of pancetta or
green streaky bacon, cut into
lardons
1 tablespoon fresh thyme leaves

16 mushrooms
2 tablespoons lemon juice
8 tablespoons walnut oil
3 bunches watercress, washed and
dried
salt and freshly ground black
pepper

Cut the backbones from the grouse. Flatten the birds and fold the wings under. Set aside about 2 dozen berries for a garnish and purée the rest through a nylon sieve. Divide the purée in half. Process half with the butter, salt and pepper. Stir 2 tablespoons of olive oil into the other half. Season the birds and cover with the raspberry-oil marinade. Leave for 1 hour.

Meanwhile if you are using streaky bacon, blanch it, rinse, and drain. Pancetta does not need to be blanched. Mix the remaining olive oil and thyme and marinate the lardons, livers, hearts and mushrooms for 45 minutes. Divide them between 8 skewers.

Preheat a grill or prepare a charcoal barbecue. Grill the grouse, breast-side down for 7 minutes, move them to a cooler part of the grill if they brown too fast. Turn them over and grill another 7 minutes. Do not overcook. Put them aside to rest for 5 minutes while you grill the skewers, turning them often.

12

Make a vinaigrette with the lemon juice, walnut oil, salt and pepper. Dress the watercress and divide between 4 warm plates. Toss the whole raspberries in the sauce remaining in the bowl and scatter around the plate. Place the grouse in the centre with a dollop of raspberry butter on top and serve.

Note: Blackberries or blueberries can be used in the same way. The recipe can also be used for other game such as quail or partridge.

Pot-Roast Grouse

serves 2

2 young grouse	finely chopped fresh herbs
1 Cox's Orange Pippin, peeled, cored and diced	2 tablespoons madeira
2 sticks of celery, diced	2 tablespoons port
unsalted butter	2 rounds of toast
	salt and pepper

Heat a knob of butter in a flameproof casserole and sauté the apple and celery until lightly coloured. Remove them with a slotted spoon to a plate. Mix another knob of butter with some herbs, salt and pepper. Place half in each of the birds' cavities. Add the oil to the casserole and sauté the birds until they are nicely browned on all sides. Return the apple and celery to the casserole, and pour over the port and madeira. Bring to a simmer on top of the stove, cover with a round of greaseproof paper and a lid and cook in a preheated oven 190°C/375°F/gas 5 for 35 minutes. Serve the grouse on rounds of toast.

Roast Grouse with Spiced Pears

serves 4

For the pears
4 ripe but firm passacrassana pears
300 ml ($\frac{1}{2}$ pint) red wine
1 stick cinnamon
5 cloves
1 teaspoon allspice berries
3 blades of mace
75 g (3 oz) sugar

For the grouse
4 young grouse, with livers
unsalted butter
2–3 tablespoons brandy
4 rounds of toast
150 ml ($\frac{1}{4}$ pint) red wine
squeeze of lemon juice
salt and freshly ground black
pepper

Peel the pears and place in a saucepan with the other ingredients. Bring to the boil and simmer, uncovered until tender. Keep turning the pears so both sides imbibe the wine and flavourings. Cool in the liquid.

Wipe the grouse and season inside and out with salt and pepper. Smear them with butter, placing a knob inside each cavity. Place them, breast-side down in a buttered roasting pan. Preheat the oven to 220°C/425°F/gas 7 and roast the grouse for 20–25 minutes. Turn them on their backs for the last 10 minutes of the cooking time.

Fry the livers in a bit of butter, keeping them nice and pink. Mash them and season. Deglaze the pan with the brandy and add to the livers. Spread on the toasted bread. Meanwhile drain and slice the pears. Reheat the pears in a low oven. Boil up the pear juices until syrupy. When the grouse are done remove them to a heated dish. Deglaze the pan juices with the wine. Add a tablespoon or two of the strained pear juices, a squeeze of lemon juice and season. Serve the grouse on the toast with some pear slices around one side. Spoon some sauce over the birds and serve.

Variations: Damsons can be spiced in the same way and are delicious with grouse. Cook them very gently so they retain their shape.

Roast Grouse à la Rob Roy

Many recipes from Scotland suggest wrapping grouse in sprigs of heather before roasting. If there is no source of heather nearby try a sprig of thyme. Apart from a knob of seasoned butter, grouse is not usually stuffed but in the Highlands a few wild raspberries, whortleberries, cranberries or rowan berries are mixed with the butter and placed in the cavity.

serves 4

4 young grouse with livers if possible,
125 g (4 oz) wild or cultivated raspberries
4 sprigs of heather or thyme soaked in a few tablespoons of whisky

4 rashers of fat green streaky bacon
1 tablespoon oil
unsalted butter
4 pieces of toast or fried bread
6 tablespoons port
salt and freshly ground black pepper

Wipe the birds inside and out but do not wash them. Mash the raspberries with 4 tablespoons of butter and some salt and pepper and divide between the cavities of the birds. Quickly sauté the livers over brisk heat in a little butter. Remove them to a bowl, deglaze the pan with 1 tablespoon of the port and add to the livers. Mash them with 1 tablespoon of butter, salt and pepper and set aside. Place a sprig of heather over the breast of the bird and secure with a rasher of bacon. Set a roasting pan on top of the stove, add 30 g (1 oz) of butter and the oil. When it begins to bubble add the grouse breast-side down. Roast in a preheated oven 220–230°C/425–450°F/gas 7–8 for 20 minutes. Remove the heather and bacon, and turn the birds breast-side up for the last 7 minutes of the cooking time. Spread the liver on the toast and set on a well heated platter. Place the grouse on top of the toast. Deglaze the pan with the port and strain over the birds. Serve at once.

Note: A little game stock (chapter 13) can replace the port if you like a purer game flavour.

PARTRIDGE

Partridge

PARTRIDGE vies with grouse for the position of premier game bird. There are two species of partridge available here; the most common is the grey or English partridge, considered to have the better and more delicate flavour. The other species is the red-legged partridge sometimes called 'the Frenchman'. This bird was introduced into Britain in the seventeenth century at a time when overshooting had threatened the British stock. It is the larger of the two birds.

To distinguish the young birds of the grey species, look for their dark beak and yellowish legs, compared to the grey beak and legs of an adult. Pointed primaries (the two outer feathers) are also an indication of youth. For the red-legged partridge these primaries will be a cream colour in young birds. The bursa test can also be applied to these birds, an inserted matchstick should go up to about 1 cm ($\frac{1}{2}$ inch) in a young bird.

The partridge season opens on the 1st of September and goes on into February. The birds should be eaten young and only hung for a few days if shot in the Autumn to preserve the delicate flavour. Older, tougher birds shot later in the season will need to be hung for around 10 days.

Young birds are best roasted, well barded with back fat. Bacon would be too assertive here. The livers are extremely delicious and should be used whenever possible, either as a stuffing or fried and spread on a croûte of bread.

———— ••• ————

Pot-Roast Partridge in Sour Cream

Soured cream is a vital ingredient of Russian cooking. It is popular with game because it acts as a tenderiser as well as providing a succulent sauce. This is a good recipe to use if you are doubtful about the age of your birds.

serves 4

4 partridge
16 juniper berries, crushed
60 g (2 oz) clarified butter
300 ml ($\frac{1}{2}$ pint) soured cream
150 ml ($\frac{1}{4}$ pint) chicken or game
   stock

2 tablespoons finely chopped
   parsley
salt and pepper
rowan jelly

Wipe the birds dry, rub them inside and out with salt and stuff the cavities with the juniper berries. Brown them on all sides in the clarified butter and place them in a casserole. Heat the stock and soured cream to just below simmering point. Pour over the partridge, cover and place in an oven heated to 170°C/325°F/gas 3. Cook very gently for about 1$\frac{1}{2}$ hours, basting at regular intervals. When the birds are cooked, remove them to a heated tin. Boil up the sauce to thicken it. Serve the partridge, with some sauce and a sprinkling of parsley. Pass the rowan jelly separately.

Grilled Partridge

serves 2

2 young partridge, plus livers
2 tablespoons lemon juice
1 tablespoon honey
2 tablespoons light soy sauce
$\frac{1}{2}$ teaspoon dried thyme

4 tablespoons unsalted butter
a glass of red wine
2 slices of toast
salt and pepper

Cut the partridge down the back to one side of the centre backbone, then cut away the backbone. Flatten out the birds and marinate for one hour in a mixture made from the lemon juice, honey, soy sauce and thyme. Heat the grill and grill them for 8 minutes breast-side down, turn over, smear the breasts with half the butter and grill for another 8 minutes or until just cooked. Adjust the distance from the heat if the partridge threaten to burn but do not overcook them. Meanwhile sauté the livers very briefly in the rest of the butter. Deglaze the pan with a splash of wine, add to the livers and mash with salt and pepper. Serve the partridge on toast spread with the liver paste. Deglaze the grill pan with the remaining wine, boil hard for a few minutes and pour over the partridge.

Partridge with Chestnuts and Cabbage

serves 6

3 partridge
200 g (7 oz) piece of pancetta or
   green streaky bacon
unsalted butter
12 small onions or shallots
a glass of white wine

6 juniper berries, crushed
300 ml ($\frac{1}{2}$ pint) well flavoured
   chicken or game stock
1 savoy cabbage
230 g (8 oz) chestnuts

Cut the pancetta into lardons and brown in a heavy frying pan. Remove them with a slotted spoon to a casserole just large enough for the birds to fit into snugly. Place a knob of seasoned butter inside each bird and brown them on all sides in the hot bacon fat. Season them with salt and pepper and place them breast-side down in the casserole. Lightly brown the shallots and add them to the casserole. Pour away the fat from the frying pan and deglaze with the wine, scraping up all the brown bits. Pour this over the birds before adding the stock and bouquet garni. Bring the casserole to a boil on top of the stove before covering the birds with a piece of greaseproof paper tucking it around the birds so it will help them self-baste. Cover with a lid and simmer it gently in a preheated oven set at 170°C/325°F/gas 3 for 45 minutes.

Meanwhile slice and blanch the cabbage in salted water for 5 minutes. Squeeze the cabbage dry and set aside. Cut a cross in the flat side of the chestnuts and drop them, several at a time, into boiling water. Remove them after 3 or 4 minutes, cut in half (this makes it easier to peel) and remove the skins. Change the water when it becomes too murky. Add both chestnuts and cabbage to the casserole

21

after the first 25 minutes of the cooking time. To serve; put the partridge on a heated dish and surround with the cabbage and chestnuts. Skim the cooking juices if necessary and boil fast for a few minutes to concentrate the flavour. Season and pour over the birds and cabbage.

Partridge with Lentils

serves 4

4 young partridge, plus livers
140 g (5 oz) small green or slate
   coloured Puy lentils
1 carrot, quartered
1 onion, pierced with 2 cloves
bouquet garni
2 tablespoons mild red wine
   vinegar
4 rashers of fat green streaky bacon

unsalted butter
2 shallots, finely chopped
2 tablespoons cognac
5 tablespoons red wine
2 tablespoons finely chopped fresh
   coriander or parsley
salt and freshly ground black
   pepper

Pick over the lentils and soak them in cold water for 1 hour. Rinse and place in a saucepan with the onion, carrot and bouquet garni. Add water to cover. Bring to a simmer, skim, and simmer very gently until the lentils are just tender. Season with the vinegar, salt and pepper.

Wipe the partridge and season. Place a knob of butter in each cavity and wrap each partridge in bacon. Smear a roasting tin with butter and set the partridge breast-side down in the tin. Place them in an oven preheated to 230°C/450°F/gas 8 and roast for 20 minutes. Turn the partridge over half way through the cooking time.

Sauté the shallots in a bit of butter until soft, add the livers and fry quickly to seal. Season and deglaze with the cognac.

Drain the lentils, discarding the vegetables and bouquet garni. Place the partridge on a heated dish and keep warm. Deglaze the pan with the red wine. Tip the lentils into the pan and heat on top of the stove. When the lentils are hot, spoon them around the partridge. Quickly heat the livers and spoon over the lentils. Garnish with coriander and serve.

Roast Partridge with Braised Curly Endive

serves 4

4 young partridge
4 pieces of pork back fat
4 vine leaves (blanched for 5
    minutes if packed in brine)
clarified butter
8 crushed juniper berries
250 g (8 oz) curly endive
100 g ($3\frac{1}{2}$ oz) spring onions,
    chopped

300 ml ($\frac{1}{2}$ pint) good chicken stock
2 tablespoons cream
a few gratings of nutmeg
2 tablespoons finely chopped
    parsley
salt and freshly ground black
    pepper

Wipe the partridge inside and out and season with salt and pepper. Place a thin piece of fat, then a vine leaf over the breasts and tie in place. Preheat the oven to 220°C/425°F/gas 7. Place a knob of butter in a roasting pan and set over heat until the butter sizzles. Add the crushed juniper berries and the birds, breast-side down. Place in the oven and roast for 20 minutes, turning the partridge on their backs after 12 minutes and removing the fat and vine leaves.

Meanwhile prepare the endive: detach the leaves, wash and dry thoroughly. Place them in a large pan of boiling salted water. When the water returns to the boil, drain, refresh under cold running water and squeeze dry. Heat 30 g (1 oz) of butter in a saucepan, stir in the onions and after a few minutes add the endive. When the endive is thoroughly soaked in the butter pour in 125 ml (scant ¼ pint) of stock. Simmer, uncovered, until the endive is tender and the stock has evaporated. Season with salt, pepper and a few gratings of nutmeg. Set aside.

When the partridge are cooked place them on a heated dish and cover loosely with foil. Degrease the pan then add the rest of the stock and boil hard until reduced to about 4 tablespoons. Strain into a small saucepan and whisk in 25 g (1 oz) of cold butter cut into small bits. Swirl the pan off and on the heat so the butter thickens the sauce rather than melts into it. Reheat the endive with a knob of butter, add the cream and parsley and season. Serve the partridge on a bed of endive with some sauce spooned over the top.

Roast Partridge with Apple, Walnut, and Madeira Sauce

serves 4

For the sauce;
2 tablespoons clarified butter
1 small carrot, chopped very fine
2 shallots, chopped fine
1 stick of celery, chopped very fine
60 g (2 oz) mushrooms, chopped
1 large Cox's orange pippin apple
1 tablespoons of lemon juice
3 tablespoons port
7 tablespoons madeira
150 ml ($\frac{1}{4}$ pint) brown chicken
   stock

12 walnut halves, skinned
30 g (1 oz) unsalted butter
salt and pepper

For the partridge;
4 young partridge
4 pieces of back fat
knob of butter
salt and freshly ground black
   pepper

To make the sauce; using a very heavy small saucepan heat the 2 tablespoons of clarified butter and add the carrots. Stir until the carrots begin to take on colour then add the shallots, celery, and a quarter of the apple cut into dice. While the vegetables are softening, peel, core and cut the rest of the apple into dice. Place in a small saucepan with the lemon juice and enough water to cover. Simmer for 5 minutes to soften the apple, then strain and keep covered until needed. When the vegetables have softened and coloured slightly add the port and 5 tablespoons of the madeira and reduce by half. Add the stock and simmer for 3 minutes. Tip into a blender and purée. Strain into a clean saucepan, pressing on the vegetables to extract as much flavour as possible. Season to taste. The sauce can be prepared up to this point several hours ahead of time.

Wipe the partridge inside and out and season with salt and pepper. Place a thin piece of fat over the breasts and tie in place. Preheat the oven to 220°C/450°F/gas 7. Place a knob of clarified butter in a roasting pan and set over heat until the butter sizzles. Set the partridge, breast side down in the pan. Place in the oven and roast for 20 minutes, turning the partridge on their backs after 12 minutes and removing the fat. Place the partridge on a heated dish and cover loosely with foil. Degrease the pan, deglaze with the remaining 2 tablespoons of madeira and tip this into the sauce. Reheat the sauce, adding the diced apple and walnuts. When the sauce is hot, whisk in the butter, a few pieces at a time, off and on the heat so the sauce thickens. Taste for seasoning. Serve the partridge with a little sauce spooned over them. A purée of celeriac (Chapter 12) would go well with this dish.

Hungarian Partridge Ragoût

serves 6

4 partridge
1 tablespoon oil
140 g (5 oz) lean unsmoked bacon,
  cut into strips
60 g (2 oz) unsalted butter
1 medium-sized onion, finely
  chopped
450 g (1 lb) mixed vegetables such
  as carrots, parsnips, celeriac,
  kohlrabi, sliced

250 g (8 oz) mushrooms, sliced
3 strips of lemon peel
300 ml ($\frac{1}{2}$ pint) partridge or
  chicken stock
300 ml ($\frac{1}{2}$ pint) soured cream
1 tablespoon arrowroot
salt and freshly ground black
  pepper
1 tablespoon of chopped fresh
  coriander to decorate

Cut the partridge into serving pieces. The carcases can be used to make the stock. Heat the oil in a flameproof casserole and fry the bacon until lightly browned. Add half the butter and onion and fry until transparent. Remove the onions and bacon with a slotted spoon and set aside. Add the rest of the butter and brown the partridge joints, then add the vegetables and mushrooms, season and stir for a few minutes to coat in the fat. Return the onion and bacon to the casserole, add the lemon peel and the hot stock. Bring to the boil, turn down the heat, cover and simmer very gently for about 45 minutes or until partridge and vegetables are cooked. Slake the arrowroot in a little cold water, stir it into the soured cream and tip into the casserole. Simmer for a few minutes, check the seasoning and serve decorated with coriander.

Pot-Roast Partridge with Shallots

serves 4

4 partridge
100 g ($3\frac{1}{2}$ oz) unsalted butter
2 tablespoons finely chopped
    parsley
1 tablespoon oil
16 large shallots, sliced

4 tablespoons brandy
4 tablespoons port
150 ml ($\frac{1}{4}$ pint) chicken stock
salt and freshly ground black
    pepper

Mix the parsley with 30 g (1 oz) of butter and season with salt and pepper. Place a knob of the parsley butter inside each bird. Add the oil with 15 g ($\frac{1}{2}$ oz) of the butter in a flameproof casserole and brown the birds all over. Remove the birds and discard the fat. Add 30 g (1 oz) of the butter to the casserole and the sliced shallots. Stir them for a few minutes to soften. Smear any remaining butter over the partridge and place them breast-side down on the shallots. Pour over the brandy and port and flame. Add the hot stock, cover tightly with a sheet of greaseproof paper and a lid. Place in an oven heated to 190°C/375°F/gas 5 for 35 minutes. Remove the partridge to a heated dish, cover loosely with foil and rest for 5 minutes. Divide the shallots between 4 heated plates and place a partridge on top.

Roast Partridge with Mushroom Sauce

serves 4

For the sauce:
45 g ($1\frac{1}{2}$ oz) dried porcini
    mushrooms (*cèpes*)
1 medium-sized carrot, finely diced
3 shallots, finely chopped
30 g ($1\frac{1}{4}$ oz) clarified butter
100 g ($3\frac{1}{2}$ oz) flat or brown-capped
    mushrooms, wiped clean and
    chopped
2 tablespoons madeira

150 ml ($\frac{1}{4}$ pint) stock or water with
    $\frac{1}{4}$ chicken stock cube
3 tablespoons whipping cream
salt and pepper
4 young partridge
1 tablespoon of finely chopped
    parsley
60 g (2 oz) butter
salt and freshly ground black
    pepper

Soak the dried mushrooms in water for at least 1 hour then strain the water through a coffee-filter paper, or muslin-lined sieve and reserve. Lightly brown the carrots in half the butter, stirring almost constantly. When they are coloured add the shallots and continue to stir until they begin to soften, then stir in the fresh mushrooms and remaining butter. Stir again adding some salt until the mushrooms give off their juices. Cook until these juice have mostly evaporated then add the madeira and evaporate. Add the stock and the soaking water, simmer a few minutes and purée in a blender. If you want a creamier sauce pass it through a chinois or fine sieve before returning it to the saucepan. Slice the dried mushrooms and add to the sauce along with the cream. Season and simmer until the dried mushrooms have softened a bit more and the consistency of the sauce is right.

Wipe the partridge dry, season inside and out with salt and pepper. Mash half the butter with the parsley, add some salt and pepper and use to stuff the birds. Preheat the oven to 220°C/425°F/gas 7. Place half the remaining butter in a roasting pan, set over heat until the butter sizzles. Smear the rest of the butter over the birds, place breast-side down in the pan and roast in the hot oven for 20 minutes. Turn the birds over for the last 7 minutes of the roasting time. Rest the birds while you reheat the sauce. Serve the partridge on a puddle of sauce. Celeriac purée (chapter 12) would go well with this dish.

Note: A good recipe to consider for entertaining, as the sauce, which is delicious, can be prepared ahead of time.

PHEASANT

Pheasant

PHEASANT are the most beautiful of all game birds. Their feathers glimmer with brilliant metallic greens, blues and rusts. The hen pheasant is speckled with rich chocolate browns and blacks. Being the most widespread of all game birds they are common sights feeding on open, cultivated land. It was thought that the pheasant originated in China, but now it is known to be European in origin and might well have been brought to these shores by the Romans, who appreciated its fine flavour. Today the pheasants in Britin are crosses between various species brought in over the years.

The first birds introduced into Britain were the black-necked species, often called the old English blackneck. The second, a Chinese sub-species, with a marked white ring around the neck. These and subsequent arrivals have interbred, creating the many variation of colouring one sees today.

As usual, the age of the bird, the length of hanging and the sex determines the taste and tenderness. Like other game birds the bursa test is the most accurate for detecting the age. In young birds, the depth of the bursa will be around 2.5 cm (1 inch), in older birds it may be completely closed, leaving a slight lump or just fractionally open. (This is tested by inserting a match). Young cock pheasants will have very blunt, short spurs compared to the long, sharp spurs of mature birds but this is not one hundred per cent reliable as spurs can become blunt with use. Hens are considered better eating than the cocks. Fresh pheasant are not in the least gamy, but have a great deal more flavour than chicken. Hanging not only helps to tenderise the meat but brings out the gaminess of the flavour. The recommended hanging time is between 7–10 days, but this depends on the weather and how strong a flavour you are after.

Braise the older birds and roast the young is long standing and good advice. Another possibility with older (and young for that matter) birds is to bone out the breast, roast or sauté it, and use another cooking method for the altogether tougher legs.

Guinea fowl, imported from France and Belgium and also bred here are available all the year round and can be used for any pheasant recipe.

Pot-Roast Pheasant with Celery and Lovage Sauce

serves 4

1 well-hung plump hen pheasant	5 tablespoons ruby port
45 g ($1\frac{1}{2}$ oz) unsalted butter	5 tablespoons madeira
2 tablespoons oil	4 tablespoons double cream
3 shallots, chopped	$1\frac{1}{2}$ teaspoons chopped lovage plus
1 celery heart, cut into thin rounds	a few leaves for decoration
150 ml ($\frac{1}{4}$ pint) game or chicken	salt and freshly ground black
stock	pepper

Heat half the butter and oil in a sauté pan. Add the shallots and stir for a few minutes until they soften. Add the celery and continue to sauté for a few more minutes. Transfer the vegetables to a casserole just large enough to hold the pheasant. Add the remaining fat to the sauté pan and brown the pheasant on all sides. Stuff a few lovage leaves inside the bird, season, and lay it breast-side down on the vegetables. Deglaze the pan with the port and madeira, boil to reduce by half then add the stock. When the stock comes to a boil, pour it over the pheasant, cover with a cartouche of greaseproof paper and then the lid. Place in an oven preheated to 180°C/350°F/gas 4 for 50–60 minutes. Remove the pheasant from the casserole and keep warm. Pour the contents of the casserole into a food-processor and whizz to a purée. Strain into a saucepan and add the cream. Bring to a simmer, stir in the remaining chopped lovage and adjust the seasoning. Serve some sauce on individual plates around the carved meat and decorate sparingly with a leaf or two of lovage.

Pheasant Legs with Mushrooms, Cranberries and Marsala

If you have used pheasant breasts for a meal this is an aromatic way of using up the legs and thighs. Serve it hot on a bed of watercress and spoon over the sauce as dressing for both meat and salad.

serves 4

4 pheasant legs and thighs	150 ml ($\frac{1}{4}$ pint) single cream
2 tablespoons oil	8 chestnuts, peeled and quartered
30 g (1 oz) unsalted butter	(optional)
2 shallots, finely chopped	16 cranberries, roughly chopped
230 g (8 oz) mushrooms, sliced	salt and pepper
100 ml (scant $\frac{1}{4}$ pint) marsala	2 bunches of watercress, washed,
150 g ($\frac{1}{4}$ pint) pheasant or chicken	dried and coarse stalks removed
stock	

Heat the oil in a sauté pan and brown the seasoned pheasant pieces. Remove from the pan. Pour away the fat, add the butter and stir in the shallots. When they are soft add the mushrooms and stir until they are coated in the fat. Return the pheasant to the pan. Pour in $\frac{3}{4}$ of the marsala and reduce by half. Add the stock, bring to a simmer and pour half the cream over the pheasant. Cover the pan and cook at the barest simmer for 30 minutes. Turn the pheasant over, add the rest of the marsala and pour over the rest of the cream. Add the chestnuts if you are using them, cover, and continue the slow cooking for another 30 minutes. Add the cranberries for the last 15 minutes of cooking time. Season with salt and plenty of freshly ground black pepper. Divide the watercress between 4 warm plates. Set a piece of pheasant over the cress and spoon over the warm mushroom and cranberry sauce.

Normandy Pheasant I

There are lots of versions of this classic French dish which combines apples, calvados and cream. The version below cooks and serves the apples separately and uses the cream and calvados for the sauce. The next recipe – Normandy Pheasant II – cooks the apples with the pheasant and the apples are sieved into the sauce. Both methods taste very good but keeping the apples separate, as below, makes a more elegant dish.

serves 6

2 pheasants
85 g (3 oz) clarified butter
150 ml ($\frac{1}{4}$ pint) pheasant or
   chicken stock
4–5 Cox's orange pippins

6 tablespoons calvados
250 ml (scant $\frac{1}{2}$ pint) crème
   fraîche, or double cream
salt and freshly ground black
   pepper

Heat half the butter in an oven-proof sauté pan or roasting tin just large enough to hold the two pheasants. Wipe the pheasants dry and brown them in the hot butter on all sides. Season them and place breast-side down in the pan. Roast in a preheated oven 190°C/ 375°F/gas 5 for 45 minutes. Meanwhile peel, core and slice the apples. Brown them in the remaining butter and set aside. When the pheasants are cooked, transfer them to a heated platter and keep warm. Heat the calvados, pour into the pan and flame it, shaking the pan until the flame goes out. Add the cream, let it bubble a few minutes, and season. Reheat the apples. Carve the pheasants and serve with the sauce and apples.

Normandy Pheasant II

serves 6

2 pheasants
4–5 Cox's orange pippins
110 g (4 oz) unsalted Normandy
   butter
4 cm (1$\frac{1}{2}$ inches) piece of
   cinnamon stick
6 tablespoons calvados
150 ml ($\frac{1}{4}$ pint) of pheasant or
   chicken stock or dry cider

250 g (scant half pint) crème
   fraîche
lambs' lettuce or watercress to
   garnish
salt and freshly ground black
   pepper

Wipe the pheasants dry, and season inside and out with salt and pepper. Peel, core and slice half the apples. Heat 30 g (1 oz) of the butter in a frying pan and brown the slices. Place them in the base of a deep casserole just large enough to hold the two pheasants. Wipe out the frying pan, add 60 g (2 oz) of butter and brown the pheasants on all sides. Flame them with the calvados, then set them breast-side down on top of the apples in the casserole. Deglaze the pan with the stock and pour over the pheasants. Cover first with a sheet of grease-proof paper and then a lid. Set in an oven preheated to 180°C/350°F/gas 4, and cook for 50–60 minutes. Meanwhile gently cook the remaining apple pieces in the rest of the butter. Remove the casserole from the oven, lift the birds on to a heated dish and cover loosely with foil. Sieve the apples and pan juices into a shallow pan. Boil vigorously, skimming off any murky bits. Bring the crème fraîche to the boil in a small saucepan and add to the sauce. Taste for seasoning. Carve the pheasants and serve with the sauce and some slices of fried apple and lambs' lettuce.

Grilled Devilled Pheasant

An easy, delicious way of cooking young pheasant. The pheasants are partially roasted then coated in mustard and breadcrumbs and finished off under the grill.

serves 4–6

2 young pheasants	4 tablespoons dijon mustard
1 clove garlic	3 tablespoons olive oil
$\frac{1}{2}$ teaspoon salt	60 g (2 oz) fresh breadcrumbs
$\frac{1}{2}$ teaspoon dried thyme	60 g (2 oz) melted butter
pinch of cayenne pepper	

Mash the garlic, salt, cayenne and thyme together in a mortar. Add the mustard and slowly work in the oil.

Cut along the backbone of the pheasant, open it out and cut away the backbone. Flatten the birds, season and brush with melted butter. Place them breast side down in a roasting tin. Roast in an oven preheated to 190°C/375°F/gas 5 for 25 minutes. Turn the pheasant breast-side up and coat with the mustard mixture. Press a layer of breadcrumbs over the mustard and sprinkle with melted butter. Place a little distance under a hot grill until the coating is well coloured. Serve immediately.

Sauté of Pheasant with Fennel and Ham

serves 6

2 pheasants, each cut into 6 pieces
2 tablespoons oil
2 tablespoons unsalted butter
4 shallots, finely chopped
3 small fennel bulbs,
300 ml ($\frac{1}{2}$ pint) dry white wine
600 ml (1 pint) pheasant or
  chicken stock
350 g (12 oz) ham, cut into 1 cm
  by 6.5 cm ($\frac{1}{2}$ in by $2\frac{1}{2}$ in) length

2 strips of lemon peel
1 bay leaf
3 tomatoes, peeled, seeded and
  chopped
4 tablespoons double cream
lemon juice
salt and freshly ground pepper

Wipe the pheasant dry and season with salt and pepper. Heat the oil in a sauté pan just large enough to hold the pieces. Sauté the pheasant pieces over medium heat, a few a time, until lightly browned. Remove from the pan and set aside. Pour away any fat.

Separate the stalks of the fennel and trim the ends. Save some of the feathery leaves for a garnish and use some to cook with the pheasant. Peel the coarse outside stalks before cutting all the stalks into batons. Add the butter to the pan and gently sauté the shallots until soft. Add the fennel and stir for a few minutes. Return the pheasant to the pan and pour in the wine. Boil hard to reduce by half. Add the ham, lemon peel, bay leaf, tomatoes and stock. Simmer, covered, until the pheasant is tender when pierced with a two-pronged fork. The time can vary from 20 minutes to $1\frac{1}{2}$ hours depending on the size and age of the birds. The wing and breast pieces will be cooked first and can be removed and set aside to keep them from overcooking. When the pheasant is cooked, return the breast and wing pieces to the pan if you have removed them, stir in the cream and simmer for minute or two. Discard the bay leaf, adjust the seasoning, adding lemon juice if needed. Serve with rice or burghul (Chapter 12).

Boned Pheasant Perigord

It really isn't hard to bone a pheasant and it can then be stuffed with something delicious and carved easily into impressive slices.

serves 4

1 pheasant
25 g (1 oz) unsalted butter
300 ml ($\frac{1}{2}$ pint) game or chicken
   stock
4 tablespoons ruby port
60 g (2 oz) small mushrooms

For the stuffing
2 shallots, very finely chopped
unsalted butter

140 g (5 oz) foie gras or calves' liver
175 g (6 oz) minced veal
3 tablespoons fresh breadcrumbs
2 teaspoons finely chopped fresh
   thyme and parsley
1 tablespoon cognac
$\frac{1}{2}$ beaten egg
salt and freshly ground black
   pepper

To bone a pheasant: Cut off the wings at the elbow, leaving the biggest wing bone on. Cut off the ankle joint on the legs. Place the bird on its breast, slit the skin down the backbone from neck to tail. With a fairly short, sharp knife, using short strokes, scrape the flesh away from the carcase, easing the skin and flesh back as you go, work on one side at a time. Cut the flesh from the sabre-shaped bone near the wing. Wiggle the wing to find the ball-and-socket joint and sever it where it meets the carcase. Do the same with the thigh bone, so that the wing and thigh are separated from the carcase but still attached to the skin. Repeat on the other side. Cut against the ridge of the backbone to free the skin, being careful not to pierce it. Hold the end of the wing bone in one hand, cut through the tendons and scrape the meat from the bone, drawing the skin inside out and using the knife to cut the bone free. Repeat the process with the thighs. Tidy up the pheasant by cutting away any excess fat and sinews. Save the bones for stock.

To prepare the stuffing:– Sauté the shallots in a knob of butter until soft. Mince or process the liver and mix with the shallots, veal, breadcrumbs, herbs and cognac. Season well and bind with the egg.

Lay the pheasant skin side down and season the flesh with salt and pepper. Heap the stuffing down the centre of the pheasant. Bring the side edges together so they meet and sew up with black thread (black is easy to see for removal).

Rub the bird well with butter and set in a roasting tin. Roast in a oven preheated to 190°C/375°F/gas 5 for 1 hour. Baste with some of the stock and the pan juices. Place the pheasant on a heated serving dish and keep warm. Tip off the fat from the roasting tin and deglaze with the port. When the port has reduced by half add the stock and reduce by half again. Taste for seasoning. Carve the pheasant into slices and serve with the sauce.

Note: The sauce can be thickened with a teaspoon of arrowroot mixed with a little cold water. Cranberry sauce (Chapter 13) goes well with this dish and looks festive.

Salmis of Pheasant with Sultanas and Mushrooms

serves 4

1 plump young hen pheasant
a handful of sultanas
$\frac{1}{2}$ cup of tea
120 g (4 oz) unsalted butter
3 shallots, chopped fine
1 clove garlic, chopped fine
$\frac{1}{2}$ bay leaf
sprig of thyme
150 ml ($\frac{1}{4}$ pint) white wine
200 ml (good $\frac{1}{2}$ pint) chicken or
    light game stock

$\frac{1}{4}$ teaspoon of quâtre-épices
3 tablespoons armagnac
400 g (14 oz) wild mushrooms,
    such as chanterelles or parasol
    mushrooms
1 tablespoon lemon juice
salt and freshly ground black
    pepper

Soak the sultanas in the tea while you prepare the pheasant. Melt half the butter in a casserole large enough to hold the pheasant. Roll the pheasant in the butter, place it breast-side down and cover with a round of greaseproof paper and a lid. Simmer it gently on top of the stove or in a low oven (170°C/325°F/gas 3) for about 45 minutes. Baste it a few times and turn it over half way through the cooking time. Remove the breast, wings and thighs and keep them warm either in a cool oven or covered loosely with foil.

Chop the carcase and add it to the casserole along with the garlic and shallots. Add the armagnac, flame it, then pour in the wine and stock. Add the spices, thyme and bay leaf. Bring to a boil, cover and simmer for 25 minutes. Meanwhile, clean the mushrooms and sweat them in a knob of butter, adding salt and lemon juice. Drain the sultanas and add them to the mushrooms. Strain the stock into a clean saucepan, pressing down on the bones and meat to extract all the flavour. Reduce the stock slightly and taste for seasoning. Whisk the remaining butter into the sauce bit by bit, and on and off the heat, so the butter thickens the sauce rather than melts into it. To serve, spoon some sauce over the pheasant and surround with the mushrooms.

Pheasant with Grapes

There is no question that grapes complement game magnificently, particularly Italia grapes, with their lovely muscatel flavour, which are available during most of the Autumn months.

serves 4

1 hen pheasant
100 g ($3\frac{1}{2}$ oz) clarified butter
250 g ($\frac{1}{2}$ lb) Italia or white seedles grapes
60 g (2 oz) breadcrumbs
4 tablespoons brandy

150 ml ($\frac{1}{4}$ pint) chicken or game stock
1 teaspoon of arrowroot
salt and freshly ground black pepper

Heat 30 g (1 oz) of the butter in an oven-proof sauté pan and brown the pheasant on all sides. Season the pheasant and place breast-side down in the pan. Roast in a preheated oven 190°C/375°F/gas 5 for 45 minutes. Meanwhile whizz half the grapes in a blender and sieve. Peel and pip the remaining grapes if necessary and set aside. Fry the breadcrumbs until golden in 60 g (2 oz) of the butter and keep warm. When the pheasant is ready, remove it from the pan to a heated dish. Add the brandy to the pan and set it alight. When the flames have died out, pour in the stock and grape juice. Scrap the bottom of the pan to loosen any bits. Mix the arrowroot with 1 tablespoon of cold water, stir into the pan, and simmer for a minute. Add the grapes. Remove the pan from the heat, season, and stir in the remaining butter to thicken the sauce slightly. Carve the pheasant and serve with some sauce and a good sprinkling of breadcrumbs.

Roast Pheasant with Onion Purée

The onion purée is really more like an onion jam and is delicious with all kinds of game. It can be served hot or cold and will keep for a week refrigerated.

serves 4

1 young pheasant, barded with
  bacon
60 g (2 oz) butter
750 g (1½ lb) onions, sliced
250 g (½ lb) cooking apples
2 teaspoons sugar

4 tablespoons dubonnet
3 tablespoons sherry vinegar
glass of red wine
salt and freshly ground black
  pepper

Place the butter in a large frying pan and heat until the butter foams. Add the onions and apples and stir until they are well coated in the butter. Cover the pan and simmer very gently for half an hour. A simmering disc is useful here as the onions should cook at the lowest possible simmer. Add the dubonnet, sherry vinegar and wine and simmer uncovered until the liquid is absorbed and the onions are almost a purée. Add a bit of water if the mixture begins to dry out before the onions are really nice and soft. Season with salt and pepper and more vinegar or sugar if necessary.

Preheat the oven to 190°C/375°F/gas 5. Place a piece of foil over the breast of the pheasant and roast the pheasant for about 45 minutes. Remove the foil and bacon for the last 10 minutes so the breast can brown. Serve the pheasant with the hot purée.

Pheasant with Cream and Juniper Berries

serves 4

1 tablespoon oil	25 g (1 oz) unsalted butter
1 tablespoon clarified butter	6 tablespoons white wine
1 pheasant	6 tablespoons game stock
1 heaped teaspoon juniper berries, chopped	4 tablespoons double cream
4 shallots, very finely chopped	salt and freshly ground black pepper

Preheat the oven to 220°C/425°F/gas 7. Brown the pheasant in the tablespoon of oil and butter in a small sauté pan. Roast it in the same pan on its breast or side for about 25 minutes. Turn the bird onto the other side half way through the cooking time. Let the pheasant rest for 10 minutes before carving.

Meanwhile sauté the shallots in the 25 g (1 oz) of butter until they are soft without allowing them to colour. Add the white wine and juniper berries and reduce by half. Add the stock and reduce by half, then stir in the cream. Deglaze the roasting pan with a little water and add to the sauce. Season to taste, then strain the sauce and serve with the pheasant.

Braised Pheasant in Cider with Walnuts

serves 4–6

2 pheasants, quartered	2 tablespoons flour
50 g (2 oz) clarified butter	2 tablespoons calvados
75 g (3 oz) walnuts, skinned	300 ml ($\frac{1}{2}$ pint) dry French cider
3 good eating apples such as Cox's orange pippins, peeled cored and sliced	150 ml ($\frac{1}{4}$ pint) double cream
	a sprig of thyme

Season the pheasant pieces and brown in a frying pan. Remove to a flame-proof casserole. Add the apple slices and walnuts to the frying pan and slightly colour them before adding them to the casserole. Place the casserole on the heat, sift the flour over the ingredients and stir to distribute. Cook for a few minutes before adding the calvados. Boil the calvados until it has evaporated, add the cider and cream and the sprig of thyme. Cover with a sheet of greaseproof paper and a lid. Place in a preheated oven 170°C/325°F/gas 3 for 35 minutes. It is crucial that the pheasant cook at the barest simmer so adjust the oven if necessary. Remove the pheasant and apple to a heated dish. Boil down the sauce to concentrate the flavour if necessary, season, and serve with the pheasant.

Pheasant with Red Cabbage and Sherry Vinegar Sauce

serves 4

375 g (13 oz) shredded red cabbage	2 tablespoons oil
85 g (3 oz) unsalted butter	3 tablespoons good sherry vinegar
2 tablespoons wine vinegar	300 ml ($\frac{1}{2}$ pint) of chicken stock or
2 tablespoons water	300 ml ($\frac{1}{2}$ pint) water with
1 pheasant, quartered, back and	$\frac{1}{2}$ chicken
wing tips saved	stock cube

Heat 25 g (1 oz) of the butter in a saucepan, add the cabbage and stir until it is well coated in the fat. Add the wine vinegar, water, salt and pepper and simmer covered over very low heat for about 15 minutes or longer if you like the cabbage well cooked. Keep an eye on it and add a bit more water if necessary. Meanwhile heat the oil and brown the pheasant pieces including the back and other bits. Lower the heat to medium and cook another five minutes on each side. They should not be completely cooked because they will finish cooking in the oven. Remove the joints but leave the extra bits in the pan. Place the cabbage in an oven dish and arrange the pheasant joints, skin side down, on top. Cover and bake in a preheated oven 180°C/350°F/gas 4 for 30 minutes.

To make the sauce, pour away any fat from the sauté pan. Add the sherry vinegar and reduce to almost nothing. Add the stock and reduce by half. Strain into a saucepan. When the pheasant is ready to be served reheat the sauce and whisk in the cold butter, a few bits at a time. This should be done moving the pan off and on the heat so the butter softens and thickens the sauce. If it becomes too hot and oily it will thin the sauce. Serve the pheasant on a bed of cabbage with some sauce spooned over.

Note: You can keep the cabbage lightly cooked and crunchy or simmer it until it is fairly soft. Either way it makes a delicious bed to serve the pheasants on.

Roast Pheasant with Coriander and Lime Stuffing

Pheasants benefit from a little stuffing placed under the skin before they are roasted. It adds flavour, helps to brown the skin and most important of all keeps the bird from drying out. Any number of different herbs or other ingredients can be used – a duxelles of mushrooms or a parsley-garlic butter for example. If you make a little sauce, carry the same flavour through in it.

serves 4

1 pheasant	1 tablespoon unsalted butter,
3 tablespoons cream cheese	softened
3 teaspoons fresh coriander leaves,	wine glass of white wine
finely chopped	200 ml ($\frac{1}{3}$ pt) good game or
$\frac{1}{2}$ teaspoon grated lime zest	chicken stock
1 tablespoon oil	salt and pepper

Preheat the oven to 220°C/425°F/gas 7. Mash the cream cheese with 2 teaspoons of the coriander and the lime zest. Season with salt and pepper. Ease the skin up from the pheasant by sliding your fingers underneath and working them around. Place a thin layer of the cheese mixture under the legs and breasts. Rub a small roasting pan with oil, place the bird on top and rub the butter over the breasts. Roast in the hot oven for 25 minutes. If the pheasant browns too quickly cover the breasts with a piece of foil. Transfer the bird to a warm dish and leave to rest while you make the sauce. Skim off most of the fat from the pan then deglaze with the wine. Reduce by half, add the stock and reduce a bit more. Season and stir in the remaining teaspoon of coriander.

Pheasant with Thyme and Redcurrant Jelly

serves 4

1 pheasant
1 tablespoon oil
1 tablespoon unsalted butter
1 teaspoon fresh thyme leaves
  (without stalks)

5 tablespoons white wine
1 tablespoon redcurrant jelly
6 tablespoons double cream
salt and freshly ground black
  pepper

Preheat the oven to 220°C/425°F/gas 7. Brown the pheasant in a mixture of oil and butter. Roast it in the oven on its side for 25 minutes, turning it to the other side half way through the cooking time. Remove the pheasant to a warm carving dish and cover loosely with foil. Allow to rest for about 10 minutes. Deglaze the pan with the wine. Add the redcurrant jelly and thyme and reduce by half. Add the cream and simmer for a few minutes to thicken slightly. Season with salt and pepper and serve with the pheasant.

Pheasant with Chicory

serves 4

1 pheasant, including neck, wing
  tips and feet
8 heads of chicory (witloof),
  trimmed
juice of half a lemon
unsalted butter
1 teaspoon sugar
1 tablespoon oil

$\frac{1}{2}$ carrot, cut into tiny dice
$\frac{1}{2}$ onion, chopped fine
1 clove garlic, unpeeled
a sprig of dried provençal thyme or
  $\frac{1}{2}$ teaspoon of dried thyme
salt and freshly ground black
  pepper

Place chicory in one layer in a saucepan. Sprinkle with salt, the lemon juice and half cover with water. Cover with a round of greaseproof paper pressed over the chicory. Simmer for about 20 minutes, turning the chicory half way through the cooking time. Drain the chicory and squeeze out the extra moisture. Return them to the pan with a knob of butter, salt and pepper and the sugar. Stir over brisk heat until they are lightly coloured then set aside. Meanwhile season the pheasant with salt and pepper and brown in 1 tablespoon of butter and oil. Remove the pheasant and discard the fat if it has burned.

Add another tablespoon of butter to the pan and add the carrot, onion, garlic, thyme, neck, wing tips and feet. Allow enough time, stirring occasionally, over gentle heat, for the vegetables to soften and become lightly caramelised. Pour 200 ml (good ¼ pint) of water over the vegetables and reduce by half. Strain, pressing down on the vegetables to extract all the flavour possible. Place the endive in a casserole with the pheasant breast-side down on top. Pour over the strained juice, cover, and set in an oven preheated to 190°C/375°F/gas 5 for 35 minutes. Remove the pheasant, rest for 5 minutes, then carve and serve with the chicory.

Note: It is crucial in this recipe to use a heavy sauté pan or saucepan, (perhaps a heavy tin-lined copper one). The vegetables can then sweat and caramelise without burning. This slow, even cooking gives the flavours time to release and water is all that is needed to deglaze the pan – a short-cut stock if you like.

Pheasant with Sauerkraut

serves 4

1 pheasant	3 carrots
900 g (2 lbs) of sauerkraut	12 juniper berries
240 g (8 oz) salt pork, or pancetta	8 black peppercorns
or speck	½ bottle Alsatian white wine
3 tablespoons goose fat or lard	4 potatoes, peeled and quartered

Cut the salt pork into lardons, place in cold water and bring to the boil. Simmer for a few minutes, skimming off any scum that rises to the surface. Drain and dry the lardons then brown them in 1 tablespoon of the goose fat. If you are using pancetta or speck omit the blanching.

Place the sauerkraut in a sieve and wash under cold running water for a minute or two then press the extra moisture out. Sauté the carrots in another tablespoon of fat then stir in the sauerkraut, juniper berries and peppercorns. Add the wine and simmer over very low heat for 1 hour. Season with salt and top up with a bit more wine if necessary. Season the pheasant and brown all over in the remaining fat.

45

Place a layer of sauerkraut in the bottom of an oven casserole, put the pheasant, breast down, on top and add the potatoes and lardons. Cover with the rest of the sauerkraut. Deglaze the pan with a bit of wine and add to the casserole. Cover the casserole and place in a very low oven for 1 hour. Cut the pheasant into serving pieces and serve on top of the sauerkraut.

Slow-Roasted Pheasant with Brazil-nut Stuffing

If you are not sure of the age of your pheasant, a safe bet is to slow roast it on a mirepoix of vegetables and stuff it to help keep it moist. Any left-over stuffing can be baked separately for the last 20 minutes of the cooking time.

serves 8

3 pheasant
60 g (2 oz) unsalted butter
3 shallots, finely chopped
1 stalk of celery, finely chopped
1 carrot, finely chopped
bouquet garni
flour for dredging
300 ml ($\frac{1}{2}$ pint) chicken or
pheasant stock
salt and pepper

For the stuffing:
5 slices of white bread, crusts
  removed
100 g ($3\frac{1}{2}$ oz) brazil nuts
60 g (2 oz) melted butter
5 tablespoons boiling water
$1\frac{1}{2}$ stalks of celery, coarsely
  chopped
1 small onion, quartered
$\frac{1}{2}$ teaspoon dried thyme
$\frac{3}{4}$ teaspoon salt
freshly ground black pepper

For the stuffing; Tear 2 slices of crustless bread into the container of a blender. Cover and blend on high speed. Empty into a bowl and repeat with the remaining bread. Grate the brazil nuts in the blender and add to the crumbs. Place the remaining ingredients in the blender and blend on high speed to a paste. Pour over crumb mixture and toss until well mixed.

Wipe the pheasant dry, season them inside and out, spoon the stuffing into the cavity of the birds, then truss. Set a roasting tin, large enough to hold the pheasants, over gentle heat, add half the butter, the shallots, carrot and celery and stir until the vegetables are golden and soft. Smear the remaining butter over the pheasants and place breast-side down on the vegetables. Tuck the bouquet garni between the birds. Roast in a 170°C/325°F/gas 3 oven for 1 hour, basting occasionally. Turn the birds over, remove the trussing strings, dredge lightly with flour, baste and return to the oven for a further 20 minutes. Remove the pheasants to a heated serving dish and keep warm. Set the roasting tin on the heat, add the stock and simmer for a few minutes, stirring to release any brown bits. Strain into a saucepan, pressing down on the vegetables to extract as much juice as possible. Adjust the seasoning pour into a heated sauceboat and serve.

Breast of Pheasant Forestière

This recipe is adapted from a dish created by chef Allan Garth when he was at Gravetye Manor in East Grinstead. The pheasant breasts are served with a pheasant mousse and a wild mushroom sauce.

serves 4

2 pheasants
1 tablespoon brandy
300 ml ($\frac{1}{2}$ pint) double cream, very cold
salt and freshly ground black pepper
unsalted butter for greasing the ramekins

For the sauce:
unsalted butter
230 g (8 oz) wild mushrooms such as chanterelles or cepès, cut in slices
300 ml ($\frac{1}{2}$ pint) game or chicken stock
6 tablespoons double cream
salt and freshly ground black pepper
pine kernels to decorate

Place a food processor bowl and blade in the refrigerator to chill.

Remove the breasts and legs from the pheasants. Set the breasts aside and bone the meat from the thighs and drum sticks. Roughly chop the meat and purée in a processor. Remove any sinews, then weigh out 140 g (5 oz) of the puréed meat and place in a bowl set over ice. Beat in the cream, a little at a time, then season with brandy, salt and pepper. Butter 4 small ramekins and fill with the mousse. Cover with foil and stand in a bain-marie of almost boiling water. Cook for

10 minutes in the oven, preheated to 190°C/375°F/gas 5, to set. Keep warm.

To make the sauce; sauté the mushrooms in the butter until they are lightly cooked. Simmer the stock and cream together until it is reduced by half, add the mushrooms, season and set aside.

Sauté the seasoned pheasant breasts in a little hot butter until lightly coloured, then put the pan into a very hot oven preheated to 230°C/450°F/gas 8 for about 5 minutes. Keep them pink so they will not be dry.

Cover the breasts loosely with foil. Reheat the sauce and adjust the seasoning. Slip a knife around the inside of the mousse and turn out on to hot plates. Slice the breasts and arrange on hot plates. Spoon some mushrooms and sauce over the breasts and decorate with a few pine kernels.

PIGEON

Wood Pigeon

ALL THE LOVELY DOVECOTS attached to grand houses and the smaller pigeon lofts on the sides of houses and barns bear witness to the past popularity of this bird. They multiplied quite happily in their round towers and enabled the owners to collect the young pigeons (squabs) before they could fly. In much the same spirit, young boys were sent up trees to wood-pigeon nests to attach strings to the squabs' legs and tie them down so they couldn't fly away.

The wood pigeon is considered the best wild pigeon for the table. It is recognised by the white ring around its neck, except when immature. A squab is a young pigeon under the age of four months, which is just the right time to eat them. The adults tend to be tough, and in my view, only the breasts are worth bothering with but they are delicious and can be treated like succulent little steaks. It is hard to distinguish the squab but the characteristics are soft red feet and downy feathers under the wings. There is no close season on pigeons so they are available all the year round. Wild pigeons are considered best during the months of May–October because many will be young and plump from the summer crops. A pigeon does not need to be hung, but the crop should be emptied immediately. If they are hung by the legs and bled for a day or so the meat will be less dark. They are not difficult to pluck, but if you have a glut of pigeons the easy way out is to peel back the unplucked skin from the breast and bone out the breast. A country friend describes this as best done over a dustbin.

Wood pigeon are freely available in Sainsbury's now. Squab that are bred for the table are available fresh in France and in America, frozen. They are starting to be bred in Britain and may well be a less rare treat in a few years time.

——— ••• ———

Pigeon Breast Salad

serves 6 as a first course

6 pigeon breasts (from 3 pigeons)
2 shallots, very finely chopped
4 tablespoons orange juice
4 tablespoons madeira
1 tablespoon mild french mustard
300 ml ($\frac{1}{2}$ pint) sunflower oil, plus
  2 tablespoons
150 ml ($\frac{1}{4}$ pint) walnut oil, plus 2
  tablespoons

24 walnut halves
60 g (2 oz) seeded raisins, soaked in
  tea then drained
a good selection of mixed green
  salad
salt and pepper
finely chopped fresh tarragon to
  decorate

For the sauce, place the shallots in a small saucepan, add the orange juice and madeira and simmer until it reduces by half. Remove from the heat. Whisk in the mustard, then gradually whisk in both oils. Season with salt and pepper.

Place the breasts between cling-film and slightly flatten, using a rolling pin, then season with salt and pepper. Heat 2 tablespoons each of sunflower and walnut oil and fry the breasts gently for about 4–5 minutes each side. Remove the breasts to a carving board and rest for a few minutes, pour away the fat from the pan, add the dressing, walnuts and raisins and whisk over moderate heat to deglaze pan and heat the dressing. Place a nice mixture of salad leaves on 6 plates. Spoon some dressing over the salad. Slice the breasts and place on top of the leaves in a fan shape. Decorate with a tiny amount of finely chopped fresh tarragon.

———— •••• ————

Peppered Pigeon Steak with Vegetables

Pigeon breasts make delectable little pepper steaks. They can be served hot for a main dish or warm as a little salad with the accompanying vegetables tossed in olive oil.

serves 2 as a main course,
*   4 as a first course*

4 pigeon breasts	4 small firm courgettes
2 teaspoons honey	150 g (5 oz) celeriac
pinch of dried thyme	3 tablespoons of groundnut oil
1½ teaspoons black peppercorns, crushed	2 tablespoons butter if serving hot, or olive oil, if serving as a salad
3 carrots	salt and pepper
4 leeks, white part only	

Gently heat the honey and thyme together. Remove the skins from the breasts and flatten between 2 sheets of cling-film with a rolling pin. Paint both sides of the breasts with the honey-thyme mixture and roll in the crushed peppercorns. Season well with lots of salt.

Cut the vegetables in thin batons all the same length and thickness. Place in a sauté pan with 6 tablespoons of water, a sprinkling of salt and the butter or olive oil. Place a sheet of greaseproof paper over the vegetables and then a lid. Simmer over very very gentle heat until the water has evaporated and the vegetables are *al dente*.

Heat the groundnut oil in a frying pan, and when it is very hot sear the breasts for about 1 minute on each side, then reduce the heat to medium and cook a further 2 minutes each side. Press down on the breasts with a spatula to help keep the shapes flat. Don't overcook them. They can be so succulent and tender if kept pink, and dry and hard if overcooked. Allow them to rest for a few minutes at least before slicing them. Arrange the slices over the vegetables and serve.

Note: If you want to prepare the vegetables ahead of time, blanch them separately, use a sieve (a chinese flat sieve is perfect) to remove them from the boiling water and set on clean drying-up cloths to cool. To reheat; place two tablespoons of wine or sherry vinegar, 1 tablespoon sugar, and 2 tablespoons light soy sauce in a large sauté pan. Add the vegetables. Place over brisk heat. By the time the liquid has evaporated, the vegetables will be hot and ready to serve.

Pigeon Breasts with Five-Spice Sauce

Sam Clark's very good five-spice sauce. The sauce can be prepared in advance leaving only the very quick frying of the breasts for the last minute.

serves 4

4 tablespoons oil
2 medium-sized onions, chopped
2 sticks of celery,
2 teaspoons five-spice powder
  (available at oriental grocers)
4 tablespoons madeira
400 ml ($\frac{3}{4}$ pint) game or chicken
  stock

2 tablespoons double cream
salt and freshly ground black
  pepper
8 pigeon breasts
very finely chopped small chives

Using a saucepan sauté the onion and celery in half the oil until soft. Stir in the five-spice powder and sauté a few seconds more then add the madeira and boil until it has evaporated. Add the stock and simmer for 5 minutes. Whizz in a blender, then strain through a chinois or other very fine sieve into a clean saucepan. Stir in the cream and reduce until it is the desired consistency. Season with salt and pepper.

Remove the skins from the breasts. Place them between 2 pieces of cling-film and flatten slightly with a rolling pin. Season the breasts on both sides with salt and pepper. Heat the remaining oil in a sauté pan and when it is very hot, seal the breasts quickly on each side, then lower the heat to moderate and give them a further 3 minutes on each side. Press them down with a spatula every now and then. Do not overcook them or they will toughen. Remove them to a warm serving dish, cover loosely with foil and rest for 3 minutes. Serve decorated with some finely chopped chives and the sauce.

— •• —

Pigeon Breasts in a Green Peppercorn Sauce

serves 4

pigeon breasts from 4 pigeons
4 tablespoons oil
5 tablespoons brandy
150 ml ($\frac{1}{4}$ pint) madeira
150 ml ($\frac{1}{4}$ pint) double cream

3 heaped teaspoons bottled green
    peppercorns
1 tablespoon oil
salt and pepper

Remove the skin and slightly flatten the breasts between 2 sheets of cling-film using a rolling pin. Season the breasts with salt and pepper. Heat the oil in a frying pan, when it is very hot sear the breasts for about 1 minute on each side then lower the heat to medium and cook for a further 2 minutes each side. This should give you pink breasts. If they are cooked to a well-done stage they will lose their tenderness and succulence. Remove the breasts from the pan and keep warm in a low oven. Pour away all but 1 tablespoon of oil from the pan. Add the peppercorns to the pan and fry for a few seconds then add the brandy and flame it. Be careful to keep your head well back and have a lid handy to cover the pan if necessary. When the brandy has reduced to about 2 tablespoons add the madeira and reduce by half. Add the cream and reduce until you have a light coating consistency, then season. This whole procedure should only take about 5 minutes – just long enough to rest the breast meat. Serve the sauce around or over the breasts.

Note: A very aromatic sauce that is made without any stock. Just the kind of thing you can whip up in minutes.

Spicy Pigeon Breasts with Coriander Sauce

Pigeon breasts cooked in this manner are like little tasty and succulent steaks and the slight coating of spices adds delicious flavour.

serves 4

For the sauce
4 pigeons
2 tablespoons oil
1 carrot, chopped
1 onion, chopped
1 stalk of celery, chopped
bouquet garni
300 ml ($\frac{1}{2}$ pint) red wine
knob of unsalted butter
2 shallots, finely chopped
6 tablespoons fresh finely chopped
   coriander leaves

3 tablespoons double cream
1$\frac{1}{2}$ teaspoons arrowroot (optional)
salt and pepper

For the breasts
2 green cardamom pods
$\frac{1}{2}$ teaspoon caraway seeds
3 teaspoons coriander seeds
grated zest from 2 limes
oil for sautéing
salt and pepper

Remove the breasts from the pigeons and set aside. Chop the carcases
and legs and brown in 2 tablespoons of oil. Add the carrot, onion, and
celery and bouquet garni and stir until they begin to colour. Add a
small glass of wine and boil hard until evaporated. Cover with water,
or stock if you have it and simmer, covered for 2–3 hours. Strain and
remove any surface fat.

   Sweat the shallot in the butter using a small heavy saucepan. Add 4
tablespoons of wine and boil hard to evaporate. Add 300 ml ($\frac{1}{2}$ pint) of
the pigeon stock and reduce by half. Stir in the coriander leaves and
simmer for several minutes. The sauce can be thickened with a little
arrowroot first slaked in water.

   Open the cardamom pods and scrape the black seeds into a coffee
grinder. Add the caraway and coriander seeds and grind. Strain the
spices through a fine sieve and mix with the lime rind and some salt
and pepper. Place the breasts between 2 pieces of cling-film and flatten slightly with a rolling pin. Cover the breasts on both sides with a
fine mixture of the spices. Heat a few tablespoon of oil in a heavy frying pan and cook the breasts over moderate heat for about 4 minutes
on each side. Rest them for a few minutes before serving with the
sauce.

——— ••• ———

Pigeon Breast in Filo

Fresh foie gras is not that easy to come by but it does make this a very memorable dish. Chicken livers may be substituted for the foie gras, but the flavour, as you would expect, is not comparable. Filo is paper-thin pastry that comes in packages containing about 12 sheets, measuring 30 cm × 48 cm (12 in × 9 in) each. It is available, usually frozen, in many supermarkets and continental stores. Thaw the filo, in its package, slowly in a refrigerator or in a cool place.

serves 8

8 pigeon breasts (from 4 wood
  pigeons)
1 large savoy cabbage
120 g (4 oz) mushrooms, very
  thinly sliced
2 tablespoons light olive oil
1 tablespoon unsalted butter
340 g (12 oz) fresh foie gras, sliced
  into 8 thin pieces

1 tablespoon flat-leafed parsley,
  finely chopped
1 tablespoon fresh coriander, finely
  chopped
1 tablespoon pine nuts, chopped
$\frac{1}{2}$ teaspoon ground cinnamon
8 sheets of filo
clarified butter, melted
salt and pepper

Separate the leaves from the cabbage, wash about 16 of them and blanch in boiling salted water until just wilted. Drain, refresh under cold running water, dry and set aside.

Remove the skin from the breasts, place the breasts between two pieces of cling-film and flatten slightly with a rolling pin. Heat the butter and oil in a heavy frying pan and lightly brown the breasts on both sides. Remove the breasts and add the mushrooms. Give them a brief sauté, then season and remove from the pan. Wipe the pan clean and dry with kitchen paper. Heat the pan and quickly sear the foie gras on both sides for a brief instant.

Cut the centre rib from at least 8 of the largest cabbage leaves. Roll up and slice another 4–5 leaves to make a little chiffonade. Mix the parsley, coriander, pine nuts, cinnamon and some salt and pepper together. Season the breast and place on a cabbage leaf. Cover with a little shredded cabbage, a few mushroom slices, the seasoning and a slice of the foie gras. Wrap in the cabbage and set to one side while you make the other parcels. Work with one sheet of filo at a time and keep the others covered to prevent them drying out. Brush the sheet with melted butter, fold it in half and wrap up the breast to make a

57

sack shape. Brush the outside with butter. Repeat with the other breasts. Bake them on a baking sheet for 10 minutes in an oven pre-heated to 220°C/425°F/gas 7. Serve with a pea purée thinned with stock made from the pigeon carcases (see Chapter 13).

Variation: If you don't want to bother with the filo the same recipe can be used for steamed pigeon parcels. Just follow the recipe up to wrapping the breasts plus stuffing, in the cabbage leaves. Make sure they are well covered in the cabbage and steam, seam-side down, in chinese steaming baskets or other steamer for about 8 minutes.

Pigeon Breast Wellington

As with most of the recipes that only use the breast, the sauce is made in advance using the carcases. These are ideal for entertaining, because the finished product is quite special and the work is largely done beforehand.

serves 6

For the sauce	2 teaspoons arrowroot
2 or 3 pigeon carcases, minus breasts	salt and pepper
3 tablespoons oil	
1 carrot, sliced	*For the breasts*
1 onion, sliced	6 pigeon breasts
1 stick of celery	450 g (1 lb) mushrooms, chopped fine
1 glass of red wine	2 shallot, chopped fine
sprig of thyme	2 tablespoons unsalted butter
1 bay leaf	a squeeze of lemon juice
mushroom trimmings (optional)	salt and pepper
5 crushed juniper berries	2 tablespoons oil
2 teaspoons redcurrant jelly	1 egg, beaten with a pinch of salt
	450 g (1 lb) puff pastry

For the sauce: Chop the carcases and place in a large heavy saucepan with the oil, carrot, onion and celery. Stir occasionally over high heat until the vegetables and pigeon take on colour. Add the wine and reduce by half. Add the thyme, bay leaf, mushroom trimmings, juniper berries and just enough water to cover. Simmer, covered, for 45 minutes, uncover and simmer another 30 minutes. Strain into a bowl, cool, and refrigerate overnight. The next day remove the fat and boil hard to reduce to about 450 ml ($\frac{3}{4}$ pint) and concentrate the flavour. Stir in the redcurrant jelly over low heat and season. Slake the arrowroot with 2 tablespoons of cold water, stir into the sauce and simmer for only a minute or two. (If you simmer the arrowroot for too long a time it will thin the sauce).

For the breasts: sweat the mushrooms and shallots in the butter until they begin to give off their juices. Season with salt and pepper and a squeeze of lemon juice. Raise the heat and cook until the juices have evaporated. Remove the mushrooms and set aside. Slightly flatten the pigeon breasts between 2 sheets of cling-film using a rolling pin. Remove the skin and season the breasts. Add the oil to the pan and when it is very hot seal the breasts quickly on both sides. Remove the breasts and leave to one side to cool while you deal with the pastry. Roll the pastry out and cut into rectangles large enough to contain a breast. Place a little layer of the duxelles on one side of the pastry, put the breast on top and cover with the remaining mushrooms. Cover with the other half of the pastry. Seal the edges with the egg wash. Refrigerate for at least 20 minutes. Bake the breasts in a preheated oven 200°C/400°F/gas 6 for 15 minutes. Let them rest for 5 minutes before serving. Arrange on plates with some sauce spooned around.

Variation: Replace the mushroom duxelles with strips of leek. Take one fat leek and cut off the green part (save this for soup). Carefully cut into the white part of the leek, lengthwise, to the centre of the leek. Blanch the leek in boiling salted water for 1 minute, refresh under cold running water. Separate the leaves of the leek and dry on kitchen paper. Use these leaves to wrap around the pigeon breast before wrapping it in pastry.

—— •• ——

Roasted Pigeon Breasts
with Sage and Bacon

It takes very little skill to bone pigeon breasts and they are surprisingly tender if cooked with care. Keep the top wing joint attached to the breasts for this recipe. This so simple it can hardly be called a recipe but it is very good.

Serves 4

breasts, with top wing joints, from
    4 pigeons
16 thin rashers of unsmoked
    streaky bacon

16 fresh sage leaves
salt and pepper

Preheat the oven to 240°C/475°F/gas 9. Season the breasts. Place a sage leaf on each side of each breast and secure them by wrapping around 2 pieces of bacon per breast. Place them in a roasting tray and roast in the top of the oven for 15 minutes. Remove from the oven, cover loosely with foil and leave to rest for 5 minutes. Serve with a vegetable purée (Chapter 12) such as swede. You could make a sauce with the rest of the pigeon but it is tasty on its own.

Pigeon Breasts with Lentils

serves 4

4 wood pigeons
4 tablespoons oil
1 carrot, sliced
1 stalk celery, chopped
1 onion, sliced
bouquet garni
4 tablespoons dry white wine
175 g (6 oz) brown or green lentils

5 tablespoons extra virgin olive oil
2 tablespoons balsamic vinegar
$1\frac{1}{2}$ teaspoons crushed black
    peppercorns
4 tablespoons fresh coriander leaves,
    finely chopped
salt and freshly ground black pepper

Carefully cut off the breasts from the pigeons and remove the skin. Slightly flatten the breasts between two pieces of cling-film. Keep refrigerated until needed.

    Chop up the rest of the pigeon carcases. Heat 2 tablespoons of the oil in a heavy frying pan and brown the bones. This can take a good ten minutes. Remove the bones to a stock pot and add the vegetables to the frying pan. Brown the vegetables in the same way. Add the wine and boil hard to evaporate before adding to the pot with the bouquet garni and enough cold water to just cover the ingredients. Bring slowly to the boil, skim if necessary, and simmer partially covered for 1½ hours. Strain, degrease, and season the stock.

Pick over the lentils, removing any small stones, and wash them. Place in a saucepan, pour over the stock and simmer, covered, for about 40 minutes. The cooking time for lentils can vary, so check after 30 minutes. They should be tender but still hold their shape. Drain the lentils and save the stock for soup. Make a vinaigrette with the olive oil and vinegar and carefully mix with the lentils. Taste for seasoning. Keep refrigerated if not using immediately. Before serving reheat in a moderate oven and decorate with chopped coriander.

Season the breasts on both sides with salt and the crushed black peppercorns. Heat the remaining 2 tablespoons of oil in a frying pan and when it is very hot sear the breasts for about 1 minute each side then reduce the heat to medium and cook a further 2–3 minutes each side. Press down on the meat with a spatula to help keep them flat. Remove from the pan and let them rest for 5 minutes before slicing and serving with the lentils.

Pigeon Croustade

serves 4

2 young woodpigeons	squeeze of lemon juice
4 tablespoons red wine	3 juniper berries, crushed
115 g (4 oz) minced veal	450 g (1 lb) puff pastry
60 g (2 oz) pork back fat, minced	1 egg beaten with a pinch of salt (egg
115 g (4 oz) mushrooms, chopped	wash)
2 shallots, finely chopped	salt and freshly ground black pepper
2 tablespoons butter	

Bone out the breasts from the pigeons, skin them and place in the red wine to marinate. Remove as much flesh as possible from the remaining pigeons and mince or process with the veal and pork fat. Sweat the shallots in the butter for a few minutes then stir in the mush-

61

rooms. Add lemon juice, salt and pepper and continue to cook until most of the moisture has evaporated. Stir into the veal mixture and season with salt, pepper and the juniper berries. Add 2 tablespoons of the red wine from the pigeon breasts.

Roll out the pastry paper-thin. Use a sharp knife and cut out 2 circles, one of 19 cm ($7\frac{1}{2}$ inches) and the other 24 cm ($9\frac{1}{2}$ inches). Use a saucepan lid or flan-tin base for a guide. Place the larger circle on a baking sheet and refrigerate. Wet another baking sheet with cold water, shake off the water but do not dry. Place the smaller circle on the damp sheet and spread with half the veal mixture leaving a clear border. Drain and dry the breasts and season lightly. Place over the meat and cover with the remaining veal. Brush the border with egg wash. Carefully place the larger circle on top and join the edges firmly with the bottom pastry. Brush the top of the pastry with the wash and make a small hole in the top. Bake in an oven preheated to 200°C/400°F/gas 6 for 10 minutes then reduce the oven to 180°C/350°F/gas 4 and bake a further 25 minutes. Serve hot.

Pigeon Breasts with Thyme Sauce

serves 4

4 pigeons	3 sprigs of thyme, fresh or dried
6 tablespoons, red wine	1 tablespoon unsalted butter
4 tablespoons olive oil	$\frac{1}{2}$ teaspoon fresh thyme leaves, finely
1 onion, sliced	chopped, or $\frac{1}{4}$ teaspoon dried
$\frac{1}{2}$ stalk of celery, chopped	1 tablespoon arrowroot
1 carrot, chopped	2 tablespoons cream
bay leaf	salt and freshly ground black
some parsley stalks	pepper

Remove the breast from the pigeons and place in the red wine to marinate. Chop three of the carcases into pieces and brown in 3 table-spoons of oil in a large heavy frying pan. Remove the pieces to a saucepan. Brown the vegetables in the frying pan and add them to the saucepan along with the bay leaf, parsley, and sprigs of thyme. Cover with cold water, bring to the boil, skim if necessary and simmer gently, covered, for $1\frac{1}{2}$ hours. Strain and reduce the stock to about 300 ml ($\frac{1}{2}$ pint) then season to taste.

Remove the breasts from the marinade and reserve the marinade. Pat the breasts dry, season, and sauté in the butter and a tablespoon of oil. They will only need about 4 minutes each side. Remove them from the pan and keep warm in a low oven. Pour off any fat from the pan and deglaze with a bit of the red wine. Add this to the stock along with the fresh thyme. Slake the arrowroot in a bit of cold water and add to the stock. Simmer for a few minutes to thicken, then stir in the cream and taste for seasoning. Serve the breasts on a pool of sauce. Vegetables such as carrots and glazed shallots would go well with this dish.

Salmis of Pigeon

Salmis appear in late mediaeval manuscripts and are still made in much the same way. Game or other meat is partially roasted then finished off in a wine sauce. It is a popular method for game birds with today's chefs who serve the roasted breasts with a quick sauce made with the remaining carcases.

serves 6

6 pigeons	2 sprigs of thyme
6 thin slices of streaky bacon	1 bay leaf
2 tablespoons oil	3 sprigs of parsley
1 carrot, finely chopped	2 tablespoons cognac
1 stalk of celery, finely chopped	400 ml ($\frac{3}{4}$ pint) red wine
5 shallots, finely chopped	1 tablespoon arrowroot
4 cloves garlic, crushed	6 croûtes fried in unsalted butter
6 black peppercorns, crushed	salt and freshly ground black pepper

Preheat the oven to 220°C/425°F/gas 7. Season the birds and place the bacon over the breasts. Roast for 8 minutes. Remove them from the oven and leave to cool completely. Remove the breasts with a sharp knife and set aside. They will be undercooked at this stage. Roughly chop the pigeon carcases and brown in the oil, either in a frying pan on top of the stove or a roasting tin set in a hot oven. Add the vegetables, and bacon and stir until they are lightly coloured. Add the herbs and spices and pour in the cognac. When it has evaporated add the red wine. Turn into a large stock pot, add water to cover and simmer for 2 hours, covered. Strain through a fine sieve and degrease. Return to a clean pan and boil hard to reduce to a good flavour.

Pour about 450 ml ($\frac{3}{4}$ pint) of the stock into a frying pan large enough to hold the breasts in one layer. Bring the stock to the boil, slip in the breasts and when the stock returns to the boil remove them to a heated dish. Add the arrowroot slaked with a little cold stock or water. Simmer for a minute or two to thicken, and adjust the seasoning. Serve the breasts on the fried croûtes with the sauce poured over.

Pigeon Breasts with Mushrooms and Raisins

serves 4

8 pigeon breasts, (from 4 pigeons)
450 g (1 lb) asorted mushrooms such as shiitake, oyster, brown-caps
45 g (1$\frac{1}{2}$ oz dried porcini (*cèpes*) small handful of seeded raisins
4 tablespoons white wine

150 g ($\frac{1}{4}$ pint) chicken stock
groundnut oil
140 g (4 oz) unsalted butter
salt and freshly ground black pepper
1 tablespoon finely chopped parsley

Soak the dried mushrooms in a few tablespoons of water for at least 30 minutes. Drain the mushrooms and strain the soaking water through a coffee filter. Soak the raisins in the wine for 30 minutes. Clean the fresh mushrooms by wiping with a damp cloth and slice into equal size pieces. Heat half the butter in a large frying pan, sauté the mushrooms, fresh and dried, with some salt and pepper until the juices start to run, raise the heat and add the soaking water. Reduce a little then add the raisins and wine. Simmer for a few minutes then strain the mushrooms and raisins over a small saucepan. Keep the mushrooms and raisins warm.

Meanwhile preheat the oven to 230°C/450°F/gas 8. Season the pigeon breasts and sauté in a few tablespoons of hot oil for a minute each side. Place them, skin-side up in a small roasting tin and roast for 5 minutes. Remove to a warm plate, lightly cover with foil and leave to rest for 5 minutes while you make the sauce. Add the stock to the saucepan containing the mushroom juices, bring to a simmer and season. Cut the remaining butter into small bits and swirl them into the sauce, off and on the heat, so the butter thickens the sauce rather than melts into it. Place some mushrooms on the centre of 4 heated plates. Set the breasts on either side and spoon some sauce over the top. Sprinkle with a tiny amount of finely chopped parsley.

Pigeon Breasts with Gingerbread Sauce

As in most of these recipes only the breasts of the wood pigeon are eaten. If you have squab the legs and thighs should also be used and the remaining carcases can go in the stockpot. *Pain d'épices* has quite a suble spicy flavour quite different from English gingerbreads. It can be found in continental grocers but if you have to settle for gingerbread adjust the amount according to how strong a ginger flavour it has.

serves 6

6 pigeons	150 ml ($\frac{1}{4}$ pint) red wine
1 carrot, chopped	3 slices of *pain d'épices* or failing
1 onion, chopped	this 1–1$\frac{1}{2}$ slices of gingerbread
1 clove garlic, crushed	1 tablespoon olive oil
1 sprig of thyme	1 tablespoon butter
$\frac{1}{2}$ bay leaf	*quâtre épices* (optional)
2 sprigs of parsley	salt and freshly ground black
4 tablespoons groundnut oil	pepper
1 tablespoon tomato purée	To decorate: fine julienne of
2 tablespoons armagnac or cognac	blanched orange peel

Remove the breasts from the pigeons. Place between cling-film and flatten slightly with a rolling pin. Set aside.

Chop the remaining carcases and place in a roasting pan with the carrot, onion, garlic, thyme, bay leaf and parsley. Add the oil and set in an oven preheated to 200°C/400°F/gas 6 for 15 minutes, or until the bones and vegetables take on colour. Be careful not to burn the bones. Pour away the oil and transfer the contents to a large stockpot. Add the armagnac and boil until it evaporates, add the wine, simmer a few minutes then add the tomato purée and cover with cold water. Bring to the boil and simmer covered, for 2 hours. Strain and leave to cool.

Degrease the stock, place in a saucepan and reduce until the flavour is good or until you have 300 ml ($\frac{1}{2}$ pint). Add the crumbled *pain d'épices* and simmer a few more minutes. Strain through a fine sieve into a clean saucepan and season.

Meanwhile season the breasts with salt and pepper or salt and *quâtre épices*. Heat the olive oil and butter in a frying pan, sauté for about 4 minutes each side. Serve on a pool of the gingerbread sauce sprinkled with the orange peel julienne.

Pigeon Breasts with Balsamic Vinegar Sauce

Here is another method of dealing with pigeon breasts, particularly good if you have to cook in advance. The entire pigeon is browned in a sauté pan and then the breasts are boned out. This keeps the breast meat underdone and it can later be finished off in a hot oven in a matter of minutes. A sauce is made with the carcases in the usual way. Balsamic vinegar is the aged *aceto balsamico*, a speciality of Modena in northern Italy. It is dark and intensely fragrant.

serves 4

4 wood pigeons, trussed	sprig of thyme
oil	1 bay leaf
5 shallots chopped	4–5 tablespoons balsamic vinegar
1 stick of celery, chopped	30 g (1 oz) butter, cubed
1 carrot, chopped	salt and freshly ground black
2 cloves of garlic, crushed	pepper
115 g (4 oz) mushrooms, chopped	

Heat a few tablespoons of oil in a large sauté pan. Season and brown the pigeons, first on one side for about 8 minutes, then the other. Let them cool down then carefully bone out the breasts and set aside. They will still be undercooked on the bone side.

Chop the carcases and brown them in the same pan. Remove them to a stockpot. Add the shallots, celery and carrots to the pan and lightly colour. Add them to the stockpot. Deglaze the pan with 3 tablespoons of the vinegar and pour into the stockpot. Add the garlic, thyme, bay leaf and enough water to barely cover the ingredients. Cover and simmer for $1\frac{1}{2}$ hours. Strain into a clean saucepan, skim, and reduce to about 300 ml ($\frac{1}{2}$ pint). If the stock has good flavour before it has reduced to this quantity, stop the reduction and freeze all but the required amount. Adjust the seasoning, adding the extra vinegar if needed. Before serving whisk in the butter over gentle heat to thicken the sauce.

Preheat the oven to 200°C/400°F/gas 6. Place the breasts in an oiled roasting tin, cover with bakewell paper and cook just long enough to finish the cooking, about 6–8 minutes. Serve with the sauce. A vegetable purée (Chapter 12) such as pumpkin or swede would go well with this dish.

Note: If you are pressed for time, a quick stock can be made in the sauté pan by browning both carcases and vegetables together, adding herbs and vinegar but only 600 ml (1 pint) of water and simmering, uncovered, for about 20 minutes.

Wood Pigeons Appleround

Here at last is a recipe using the entire wood pigeon given to me by Caroline Hobhouse.

1 young pigeon per person	celery
4–6 hunza apricots per pigeon, soaked in weak China tea	stock
	a glass of gin
350 g (12 oz) piece of lean smoked bacon. (enough for 4–6 birds), cubed	red wine (optional)
	bouquet garni
	unsalted butter
2 crushed garlic cloves	salt and freshly ground black
onions	pepper.
carrots	

Deprive the birds of life and feathers, and gut them. Season the cavity and put in 4–6 stoned apricots (saving the soaking liquor).

In a heavy casserole large enough to hold all the pigeons on end in one layer, brown the cubes of lean smoked bacon in a little oil, then sweat the garlic and enough chopped onions, carrots and celery to make a 2 cm ($\frac{3}{4}$ inch) layer. Put in the birds. Pour over a glass of warm gin and flame. Add the apricot soaking water, some red wine if wanted and enough stock to cover. Add the bouquet garni. Bring to a boil and transfer to a medium oven 400°F/200°C/gas 6 for

$1\frac{1}{2}$ hours or a cooler oven for a longer time (The latter if you are doubtful about the age of the pigeons). Season with salt and pepper and a squeeze of lemon before serving with plain steamed celery tossed with butter and pepper. The sauce can be boiled down to thicken if wanted.

Note: Save the carcases off your guests' plates. They, and the remaining juices and vegetables can make a good game soup.

Roast Squab

Squabs are excellent simply roasted and served with the pan juices or a little madeira sauce.

serves 6

6 squab	6 tablespoons madeira
3 tablespoons clarified butter	60 g (2 oz) chilled butter, cubed
450 ml ($\frac{3}{4}$ pint) game or chicken stock	salt and freshly ground black pepper

Heat the oven to 220°C/425°F/gas 7. Place the clarified butter in roasting pan and, set in the oven until the butter sizzles. Meanwhile wipe the birds dry and season. Place the birds, breast-side down in the hot butter and roast for 10 minutes. Turn the birds over, baste and roast for another 10 minutes. Set the squabs on a heated dish and cover loosely with foil. Degrease the pan then deglaze with the madeira and reduce by half. Add the stock and reduce slightly. Whisk in the butter gradually, on and off the heat to thicken the sauce. Season with salt and pepper. Serve with glazed onions and swede or butternut squash purée.

Squab can also be roasted whole with a stuffing of cream cheese, herbs and apricots.

Note: If you are trying to cut down on butter you can thicken the sauce with 2 teaspoons of arrowroot slaked in a little cold water and simmered in the sauce for a minute or two.

68

WOODCOCK, SNIPE AND WILD DUCK

Woodcock, Snipe and Wild Duck

WOODCOCK (which belong to the same family as snipe) are waders and live in damp woods on a diet of berries, insects and worms. In Britain most woodcock are sedentary but those which live further north in Europe regularly migrate southwards to North Africa.

There are three varieties of snipe but the most likely one to end up in the game bag is the Common Snipe. It is common only in the sense that it is widely distributed – from Ireland to Japan. It nests in this country but its numbers are increased by visitors in autumn and winter. It lives in damp inland haunts, but in hard winters it may move to the shore. It probes the marshy terrain with its long bill for worms and insects. The Great Snipe is a rare visitor that stops occasionally on its migratory journey, but does not nest in this country. The smaller Jack Snipe nests in Scandinavia, northern Russia and Siberia and comes to Britain in the winter.

Woodcock is prized for its fine flavour and considered to be at its best between October and December; it is hung from 3–8 days. Snipe are at their peak in the winter, and are eaten fresh or hung for a few days. Both birds need to be carefully plucked, including the head which is left on when cooked. They are cooked undrawn (because the entire contents of the gut is excreted when they take to the wing) and only the gizzard is removed. When the birds are cooked the entrails or 'trails' are spooned out and spread on toast, or made into a sauce. If the birds are well roasted, the trails largely melt into the pan juices. After the birds are cooked the heads can be split open to expose the very edible brains. The birds can also be roasted drawn, the trails fried up in a little butter and herbs, then spread on toast and served with the birds.

Mallard, teal, widgeon and pintail are the most usual of the wild ducks eaten in Britain, mallard being the most common and widely distributed in the Northern Hemisphere, and the most likely wild duck to be found in the market. The tiny teal is considered by many to have the finest flavour. It also presents a great challenge for the marksman because of its size and speed. Any duck shot in marshy coastal areas may have picked up a fishy flavour while feeding and can be marinated in milk and orange juice for several hours. Young ducks are, of course, the best to eat and can be identified by having pinker feet and brighter bills than the older birds. The best time to eat duck is in the autumn when they are plump with fatty reserves for the winter ahead. The maximum they should be hung is 2–3 days, but they are usually eaten fresh.

An interesting development on the duck scene is the Gressingham duck, a cross between a mallard and a domesticated duck, now being farmed by Peter Dodd in – Lancashire – the trend is likely to grow with the advantages of plump tenderness and good flavour that a cross-bred bird can produce.

——— •●• ———

Roast Woodcock

Pluck the birds carefully to avoid breaking the skin. Skin the heads and remove the gizzard but leave the rest of the innards. Truss them with their beaks to one side, season, and bard with a thin strip of back fat or slice of fat bacon. Roast in an oven preheated to 230°C/ 450°F/gas 8 for 18 minutes. Remove the fat for the last 5 minutes of the cooking time to brown the breasts. Serve on a croûte of fried bread. The innards can be mashed up and heated with any pan juices, salt and pepper, and a few drops of brandy then spread on the croûte as a seat for the bird. The heads can be split open to expose the edible brain. Alternatively any pan juices can be poured over the croûtes and the birds can be served intact and dealt with by the individual diners.

——— •●• ———

Woodcock with Foie Gras

serves 4

4 woodcock, ungutted except for
  gizzard
4 thin squares of back fat or fat
  bacon
100 g ($3\frac{1}{2}$ oz) clarified butter

100 g ($3\frac{1}{2}$ oz) foie gras or 2 oz (60 g)
  chicken livers
3 tablespoons armagnac
8 thin rounds of white bread
salt and pepper

Season the birds, truss and bard them with the fat. Place in a well
buttered oven pan and roast for 10 minutes at 220°C/425°F/gas 7.
Remove from the oven, take off the fat and trussing string. Split the
birds in half, spoon out the innards and set aside. Return the woodcock halves to the oven and roast for another 10 minutes. Meanwhile
mash the innards with the foie gras, add 1 tablespoon of the armagnac
and season with salt and a good bit of black pepper. Fry the bread in
the remaining butter, drain and keep warm. When the birds have
finished cooking, remove them from the oven and keep warm.
Degrease the pan, add the rest of the armagnac and boil for 1 minute.
Add the foie gras mixture and cook the sauce, stirring, for a few
minutes, until the sauce loses its red colour. To serve: put two rounds
of bread on each heated plate, spoon over some sauce and set the half
birds on top.

Grilled or Roast Snipe

1–2 per person

Snipe are prepared for cooking in the same way as woodcock. Their
smaller size makes them ideal for grilling or spit-roasting in front of a
fire. Season the birds, coat with butter and bard with a thin piece of
back fat or thin rasher of streaky bacon over the breast. Grill them a
little distance from the heat source so they won't burn. Alternatively
roast them in an oven preheated to 220°C/425°F/gas 7 for about 12
minutes. The innards can be mashed in the pan juices, heated to
below the boil, seasoned, and served on fried bread.

Wild Duck Breasts with Blueberry Sauce

The sauce is a beautiful red plum colour and very good with duck.

serves 4

150 g (5 oz) blueberries or
    bilberries
1 tablespoon lemon juice
1 tablespoon sugar
4 duck breasts, boned but with
    skin left on

1 tablespoon olive oil
150 ml ($\frac{1}{4}$ pint) good red wine
250 ml (scant pint) well flavoured
    duck or chicken stock
salt and freshly ground black
    pepper

Wash and drain the blueberries. Place 125 g (4 oz) of them in a small saucepan. Mash the berries with a fork, add the lemon juice, cover, and cook at the lowest possible heat to just soften the berries. Add the sugar and cook covered for another few minutes then remove from the heat.

Meanwhile heat the oil in a heavy sauté pan. Prick the skin of the breasts and lightly season. When the oil is good and hot place the breasts skin side down in the pan and sauté for 6 minutes. Turn the breasts over and cook a further 5 minutes, or until the breasts have firmed up somewhat but still have some bounce when pressed with a finger. Remove the breasts to a warm plate and keep warm either in a low oven or under foil. Pour away all the fat from the pan. Add the red wine, bring to a simmer and reduce by half. Pour the stewed berries into a very fine sieve and sieve a good half of the mixture directly into the pan. Add the stock and simmer for a minute or two. Taste for seasoning, adding more of the sieved berries as necessary. Once the sieved berries are added to the stock do not simmer longer than necessary, or the fruit flavour will be impaired. Add the reserved whole berries to the sauce. Serve the breasts in a pool of sauce.

Breast of Wild Duck with Champagne Vinegar Sauce

serves 4

4 duck breasts, boned but with the
   skin left on
1 tablespoon caster sugar
6–7 tablespoons champagne
   vinegar

600 ml (1 pint) duck stock made
   from carcases (Chapter 13)
70 g (2$\frac{1}{2}$ oz) cold unsalted butter
salt and freshly ground black
   pepper

Place the breasts in a heated non-stick pan, skin side down. Cook for 10 minutes over medium-hot heat (the skin should not burn), turn over and cook for 3 minutes more. Keep warm in a low oven between two plates, to relax the meat, while you make the sauce.

Pour away fat from pan. Sprinkle on the sugar and heat gently until it carmelises. Deglaze with the vinegar and reduce by half. Add the stock and reduce until the flavour seems right, then season. Cut the butter into cubes and whisk it in over low heat or off the heat so the butter thickens the sauce. Serve with potatoes, fried in duck fat if possible, and apple wedges.

——— •●• ———

Wild Duck Breast with
Cherries and Cardamom

The combination of morello cherries and cardamom is used in a Russian recipe for veal but it is equally good with duck. The legs of the duck are removed before the duck is roasted so the breasts can be done '*à pointe*' and the legs dealt with for another occasion.

serves 6

3 mallard ducks
4 tablespoons butter
2 tablespoons flour
600 ml (1 pint) duck or chicken
  stock
550 g (1¼ lb) morello cherries,
  fresh or bottled
6 spring onions, finely chopped

90 g (3 oz) sultanas
small glass of tawny port
6 green cardmom pods, crushed
sugar, salt and freshly ground
  black pepper
chopped chives to decorate.

Preheat the oven to 240°C/475°F/gas 9. Remove the legs from the ducks and save for another meal. Season the rest of the duck with its breast intact and roast, breast-side down, on a buttered roasting tin for 20 minutes. Meanwhile make the sauce; (it can also be done in advance). Stone, and stew with a little water until tender, or drain and stone preserved cherries, reserving the juice. Heat the butter in a heavy saucepan and stir in the spring onions. When they are soft, stir in the flour. Add the port and ¾ of the stock, whisk until the stock simmers, then add the cherries, cardamom pods and 3 tablespoons of cherry juice. Simmer uncovered, for 20 minutes. Taste for seasoning adding more stock, cherry juice or sugar, salt and pepper as needed. When the breasts are done place them on a heated dish and cover loosely with foil. Pour off the fat from the tin, deglaze with some sauce and pour this back into the rest of the sauce. Carve the breasts into slices, spoon a ring of sauce around, and decorate with the chives.

——— •●• ———

Mallard Duck Breasts with Pomegranate Sauce

Pomegranates and wet (fresh) walnuts appear in November and combine beautifully in a sauce for wild duck.

serves 4

2 mallard ducks	a pinch of thyme
2 small onions, unpeeled and sliced	3 ripe pomegranates
2 carrots, chopped	12 wet (fresh) walnuts
1 stalk of celery, chopped	2 tablespoons oil
6 tablespoons light olive oil	1 tablespoon arrowroot
a glass of red wine	salt and pepper
1 bay leaf	

Carefully remove the breasts from the ducks and set aside. Remove the legs with the thighs, cut off the wings and chop the carcases. Place all the pieces of duck except the breasts in a heavy saucepan, add the vegetables and half the oil and sauté over high heat for about 15–20 minutes, or until the duck and vegetables are nicely browned. Add the wine and boil until it has evaporated. Add the thyme, bay leaf and just enough water to barely cover the duck. Boil for 20 minutes, then strain into a bowl. The stock should have quite a good flavour even in this short cooking time. Degrease the stock (reduce if necessary), season lightly and set aside. Add more water to cover the duck, bring to the boil and simmer for another hour. Remove the legs and thighs when tender. The meat can be removed from the legs and thighs and processed with butter, a few tablespoons of stock, and salt and pepper to make a delicious little duck paste. This second stock can be strained, degreased and frozen for another use. Meanwhile cut the pomegranates in two, scoop out a few tablespoons of the seeds and set aside. Squeeze the rest of the halves in an orange squeezer and strain the juice. Crack open the walnuts and peel the walnut halves. If the walnuts are wet the skin is easy to peel. If you are using ordinary dried walnuts, drop them in boiling water for 30 seconds, then peel with fingertips or a toothpick. Slightly flatten the duck breasts between cling-film using a rolling pin. Heat the remaining oil in a heavy frying pan, season the breasts and sauté skin-side down for about 8 minutes, turn over and sauté for a further 5 minutes. Alternatively roast them skin-side up in an oven preheated to

220°C/425°F/gas 7 for 12 minutes. Pour away the fat, deglaze with 250 ml (scant ½ pint) of stock and add a good half of the pomegranate juice and the walnuts. Simmer a minute or two and taste. Add the rest of the juice if the sauce needs it and season with salt and pepper. Slake the arrowroot in a 2 tablespoons of cold water, add to the sauce and simmer for 1 minute. Add the reserved pomegranate seeds. Serve the breasts well covered with sauce.

Note: The stock can be prepared in advance. If you prefer to cook the breasts before your guests arrive, roast them for only 10 minutes, several hours ahead of time, slice when cold and reheat for barely 30 seconds in the hot sauce.

Wild Duck with Citrus Fruit

serves 4

3 navel oranges	3 tablespoons caster sugar
1 lemon	150 ml (¼ pint) good duck or
1 lime	chicken stock
2 young wild ducks	2 teaspoons arrowroot
60 g (2 oz) clarified butter	1–2 tablespoons grand marnier
3 tablespoons cognac	salt and freshly ground black
2 tablespoons red wine vinegar	pepper

Using a potato peeler, peel off the zest in large strips from one of the oranges, the lemon and lime. Chop one strip of the orange rind and mix with a small knob of butter. Cut the remaining rind into fine julienne. Blanch them for 8 minutes in boiling water, drain, refresh under cold running water and set aside. Squeeze the juice from the pared fruit and reserve. Cut peel and pith off the remaining two oranges, discard, and cut flesh into segments.

Season the ducks inside and out and stuff with the orange butter. Preheat the oven to 200°C/400°F/gas 6. Heat the remaining butter in a roasting tin, place the ducks breast side down in the hot butter and roast for about 50 minutes. Baste frequently and turn the ducks breast side up for the last 10 minutes of the cooking time.

While the duck is roasting place the sugar and one tablespoon of water in a small heavy saucepan and cook the sugar until it caramelises. Remove the pan from the heat and pour in the vinegar. Avert your face while you are adding the vinegar because it can spit on contact with the very hot syrup. Set the pan back over the heat and stir to dissolve the caramel. Pour in the stock and season. When the ducks are cooked heat the cognac, pour over the birds, flame, and shake the pan until the flames die away. Remove the ducks to a hot serving dish and cover lightly with foil. Skim off most of the fat from the pan and add the pan juices to the caramelised sugar. Slake the arrowroot with 2 tablespoons of cold water, stir into the pan and bring to a boil. Add $\frac{1}{2}$ of the fruit juice, the julienne, and grand marnier. Taste, add more juice if needed and adjust the seasoning.

Carve the ducks, serve with the sauce decorated with the heated orange slices.

Note: If you want the breasts to be nice and pink, cook the duck for 10 minutes less. After the breasts are carved the rest of the duck can be returned to the oven to cook further. The legs can be served for second helpings.

Wild Duck with Turnips

serves 4

2 mallard, trussed	450 g (1 lb) turnips
1 tablespoon oil	a large pinch of sugar
25 g (1 oz) unsalted butter	4 tablespoons madeira
1 tablespoon flour	1 tablespoon of finely chopped
500 ml (scant pint) chicken stock	chervil
bouquet garni	salt and pepper
16 small pickling onions or shallots	

Heat the oil with 1 tablespoon of butter in a casserole and over a gentle heat slowly brown the ducks on all sides. This will take about 15 minutes. Remove the ducks and pour away all but 2 tablespoons of the fat. Add the flour to the pan and stir, always over a gentle heat, until the flour lightly browns. Don't allow it to burn. Stir in the stock, bouquet garni, pepper and salt if the stock was unsalted. Simmer stirring for a few minutes. Replace the ducks, cover with a sheet of greaseproof paper pushed well down into the casserole and cover with a lid. Place in a preheated oven 150°C/300°F/gas 2 for 20 minutes. The heat should just allow the ducks to cook at the merest simmer.

Meanwhile prepare the turnips by peeling, and leaving whole if small, or quartering and shaping into ovals if large. Heat the remaining butter in a frying pan and sauté the shallots until coloured. Remove them from the pan and add the turnips and sugar. Sauté until the turnips have also browned. When the duck has had its 20 minutes oven time, add the turnips and shallots to the casserole, basting them with the liquid. Re-cover with both paper and lid, return to the oven, and cook gently for another 30 minutes.

Transfer the ducks to a hot dish. Use a slotted spoon to spoon the vegetables around the ducks. Bring the sauce to a boil, add the madeira and adjust seasoning. Spoon some sauce over the duck, sprinkle the chervil over the vegetables and serve the remaining sauce separately.

Braised Wild Duck with Onions and Apples

serves 6

2 mallard ducks
1 onion, stuck with 2 cloves
    and halved
60 g (2 oz) unsalted butter
2 tablespoons oil
3 medium onions, thinly sliced
1 large cooking apple, peeled,
    cored and sliced

2 Cox's eating apples
600 ml (1 pint) French dry cider
1 teaspoon sugar
150 ml ($\frac{1}{4}$ pint) double cream
2 tablespoons calvados
salt and pepper

Season the ducks inside and out and stuff with half an onion. Heat half the butter with the oil in a heavy frying pan and brown the ducks on all sides. Remove the ducks and set aside. Add the onions to the pan and sauté for about 15 minutes, stirring, then add the slices of cooking apple and stir a few more minutes. Season well with salt and pepper. Place the onion-apple mixture in a heavy flame-proof casserole large enough to hold the two ducks snugly. Place the ducks on top, breast-side down and pour over the cider. Bring to the boil, cover tightly and simmer very gently for 1 hour. Meanwhile peel, core and slice the eating apples. Sauté them in the remaining butter and the sugar until soft and lightly coloured, keep warm.

Heat the calvados, pour over the ducks, and flame. Remove the ducks to a heated dish and cover loosely with foil. Degrease, boil the sauce to concentrate the flavour, stir in the cream, simmer a few minutes and taste for seasoning. Carve the ducks, and serve with the onion sauce and decorate with the apple slices.

Wild Duck Breasts with Rosemary Sauce

serves 6

6 wild duck breasts, (from 3 ducks)
sprig of rosemary
1 tablespoon very finely chopped
    fresh rosemary
1 tablespoon unsalted butter
1 shallot, very finely chopped
$\frac{1}{2}$ carrot, very finely chopped
$\frac{1}{2}$ stalk of celery, very finely
    chopped

small glass of white wine
300 ml ($\frac{1}{2}$ pint) duck stock
    (Chapter 13)
squeeze of lemon juice
1 tablespoon arrowroot
1 tablespoon port
salt and freshly ground black
    pepper

Score the duck skin and rub with salt and pepper; place in an oiled tin with a sprig of rosemary on top. Roast in an oven preheated to 215°C/425°F/gas 7 for 15 minutes.

While the duck is roasting sauté the vegetables in the butter, stirring, until softened. When the breasts are done remove them to a serving dish and keep warm. Pour off any fat from the roasting tin and deglaze with the wine. Add to the vegetables and simmer until slightly reduced. Add the stock and chopped rosemary, and reduce slightly. Mix the arrowroot with the port and 1 tablespoon of water, add to the sauce, and simmer for a minute or two. Taste for seasoning, adding lemon juice if necessary. Pour some sauce on to hot plates and set the breasts on top.

Teal with Seville Orange Sauce

serves 4

4 teal	2 tablespoons flour
3 large seville oranges	3 tablespoons red wine
1 navel or other eating orange,	300 ml ($\frac{1}{2}$ pint) duck or game stock
unsalted butter	3 tablespoons grand marnier

Use a potato peeler to peel the skin in strips from two well washed, seville oranges. Cut into fine julienne and blanch in a large quantity of boiling water for 8 minutes. Refresh under cold running water and drain. Squeeze the juice from all 4 oranges and set aside.

Heat 3 tablespoons of butter in a heavy saucepan until it froths, add the flour and cook until the butter turns a light golden brown. Whisk in the stock and wine, and continue to whisk until the sauce is smooth. Simmer for 5 minutes. The sauce can be made in advance up to this point. A piece of cling-film floated over the surface will prevent a skin forming.

Wipe the teal dry and season inside and out with salt and pepper. A little of the julienne and a knob of butter can be placed in the cavities. Heat the oven to 230°C/450°F/gas 8. Rub the breasts with a little butter and roast for about 12–15 minutes, basting with a little orange juice half-way through the cooking time. Heat the grand marnier, pour over the ducks and flame. Remove the ducks from the pan and keep warm. Pour away the fat from the pan and deglaze with more of the orange juice. Pour this into the sauce and reheat, adding the rest of the orange juice and the julienne. Adjust the seasoning and serve with the teal.

——— •●• ———

Roast Teal

one teal per person

unsalted butter
petit suisse
thyme
seasoned flour

duck or game stock or red wine or port
salt and freshly ground black pepper

Preheat oven to 230°C/450°F/gas 8. Wipe the teal dry and season with salt and pepper. Stuff each teal with a knob of butter or petit suisse seasoned with herbs, salt and pepper. Butter a roasting tin, set the teal on top breast-side down, and roast for 15–20 minutes. Turn the birds over half-way through the cooking time, dust lightly with flour and baste with the stock or alcohol. Make a little gravy with the pan juices while you rest the birds for 5 minutes, covered loosely with foil.

Note: If the teal were shot in marshy coastal areas marinate for 5 hours in milk, orange juice and herbs to help get rid of any possible fishy flavour.

QUAIL

Quail

IT IS still just possible to hear the call of the of wild quail in southern England during May and June, though your chances vary from year to year depending on the numbers of these small visitors that are about. They favour chalk grasslands but are difficult to spot in the countryside because they prefer to run hidden among the grasses and hedgerows. When they fly they resemble the partridge, flying very low and for short distances. Quail is the smallest European game bird and the only truly migratory one. It winters in Africa and India but breeds in Europe. At one time considerable numbers nested in the British Isles but vast numbers of quail were netted and shot on their migratory journeys. The population was reduced so dramatically that they became protected birds in Great Britain, although they are still shot in Europe. Before the Second World War the majority of quail for sale in England were netted in Egypt and imported alive to this country where they were fattened before being killed. Today the quail you buy is farmed in this country and is often the Japanese species. It is bred domestically for both eggs and birds. The hens' broodiness was bred out by the Japanese, so hatching takes place in incubators. The eggs have charming patterns which are unique to each bird.

Although the birds are so tiny that you need two per serving they have very light bones – a characteristic of migratory birds. Three-quarters of their weight is meat. Farmed quails are not hung, but eaten fresh. They are also sold partially boned but, although a convenience, it is not always well done commercially. It takes little skill to bone out the breasts at home and the birds will end up looking neater and the bones can provide the stock. Farmed quail have a delicate flavour and are very tender. It is hard to toughen them, no matter what cooking method you use. With their diminutive size they can be attractively served in mushroom caps or peppers and can be an inspiration for the creative cook.

—— ••• ——

Quails Braised in Wine with Ham

A very easy, quick recipe which has the added advantage of not needing stock. For a more substantial dish you could serve the quail on fried croûtes or grilled bread rubbed with garlic and sprinkled with good olive oil.

serves 4

8 quail
60 g (2 oz) unsalted butter
2 tablespoons olive oil
230 g (8 oz) ham, cut into lardons
120 g (4 oz) small button
   mushrooms

4 juniper berries, crushed
$\frac{1}{2}$ bottle of dry white wine
salt and pepper

Heat the butter and oil in a heavy sauté pan large enough for the quails to fit in one layer. Season the quails and brown on all sides. Add the ham, mushrooms and juniper berries to the pan then pour over the wine and bring to a boil. Lower the heat so the wine is at a bare simmer, cover the quails with a sheet of greaseproof paper and then a lid. After 15 minutes turn the quails over, re-cover, and continue to cook gently for another 15 minutes. Remove the quails to a heated serving dish and keep warm. Reduce the cooking juices, taste for seasoning, and serve with the quail.

——— •●• ———

Braised Quail with Polenta

Polenta is a favourite accompaniment for game in Italy and it is excellent with quail cooked in this Italian manner.

serves 4

8 quail
8 fresh sage leaves, chopped
2 tablespoons olive oil
3 tablespoons butter
8 fresh sage leaves, chopped
60 g (2 oz) pancetta or unsmoked
    bacon, cut into lardons

300 ml ($\frac{1}{2}$ pint) white wine
150 ml ($\frac{1}{4}$ pint) chicken stock
salt and freshly ground black
    pepper
grilled polenta (Chapter 12)

Season the insides of the quails with salt and pepper and a pinch of the sage. Heat the oil and one tablespoon of the butter in a flame-proof casserole or sauté pan with a lid. Add the pancetta and stir for a minute or two, then add the quails and brown on all sides. Season the quail with salt and pepper. Pour away any fat from the pan, add half the wine, reduce slightly then add the stock. Lower the heat until the liquid is just barely simmering, cover, and cook for about 35 minutes, turning the quail occasionally. Remove the quail to a warm serving dish. Deglaze the pan with the remaining wine, taste for seasoning and stir in the remaining butter off the heat to thicken the sauce. Pour over the quail and serve with grilled polenta.

——— •●• ———

Babette's Quail

The centrepiece of the extraordinary meal, in the film *Babette's Feast*, based on a story by Isak Dinesen was 'caille en sarcophage' – quail stuffed with foie gras and served in a puff pastry nest. It made me long to taste it and this is my attempt to do so. Babette's version included truffles. You will probably find foie gras luxurious enough.

serves 6

450 g (1 lb) puff pastry, preferably home-made
1 egg beaten with a pinch of salt

For the sauce
15 g ($\frac{1}{2}$ oz) butter
4 shallots, finely chopped
115 g (4 oz) brown capped mushrooms, very finely chopped
3 tablespoons ruby port
4 tablespoons dry madeira
300 ml ($\frac{1}{2}$ pint) brown chicken stock

3 tablespoons cream
2 teaspoons arrowroot
salt and freshly ground black pepper
6 large quail
400 g (14 oz) fresh foie gras
25 g (1 oz) butter
340 g (12 oz) brown capped mushrooms, finely chopped
2 tablespoons parsley, very finely chopped
3 tablespoons cream
salt and pepper

First make the pastry cases; roll out the dough to a thickness of a little less than 5 mm ($\frac{1}{4}$ inch) and cut it into ovals approx 10 cm × 12 cm (4 × 4$\frac{3}{4}$ inches) Place them on dampened baking sheets and brush with egg glaze. Using a sharp knife trace a line about 1.25 cm ($\frac{1}{2}$ inch) from the edge of each oval, without cutting all the way through the pastry. Make a simple bird or feather design on the inside oval. This is optional but will add charm to the final dish. Chill the pastry for 15 minutes then bake in an oven heated to 220°C/425°F/gas 7 for about 18 minutes. With a knife, cut around the inside ovals, lift them out and set aside. Scoop out any uncooked dough from the large cases. Remove both cases and lids to a rack to cool.

For the sauce, sweat the shallots in the butter for 4 minutes, stirring, without allowing them to colour. Add the mushrooms and cook for a further few minutes. Add the port and madeira, simmer a minute or two before adding all but a few tablespoons of the stock. Simmer for 15 minutes then strain through a fine sieve into a clean pan, pressing on the vegetables to extract all the juices. Adjust the seasoning and set aside.

Slice the foie gras into 8 mm ($\frac{1}{3}$ inch) slices, and season lightly. Heat a non-stick frying pan until it is very hot and sear the slices very quickly on both sides. Remove from the pan. Drain off all but a few tablespoons of fat. Add the mushrooms to the pan and saute until they are lightly cooked. Stir in the parsley and cream. Cut the liver into 2.5 cm (1 inch) cubes, add to the mushrooms and season.

Make a slit down the back of each quail and bone out the centre bones. Leave the legs intact. Lightly season the quails, place some foie gras stuffing in the centre and sew up the quails. (Use black thread for easy removal) Tie the legs together to keep a neat shape. Smear a little butter over the breasts of the quail and roast in an oven preheated to 230°C/450°F/gas 8 for 15 minutes. Remove the quails from the oven, cover loosely with foil and leave to rest. Pop the pastry cases and lids back in the hot oven to reheat. Degrease the roasting pan then deglaze it with some of the sauce. Add this to the rest of the sauce, bring to a simmer then add the cream. Slake the arrowroot in the remaining stock, stir into the sauce and simmer for a few minutes to thicken the sauce.

Remove the thread from the quails. Place a pastry case on a heated plate, set a quail inside and spoon over a few tablespoons of sauce. Lean the pastry lid against the nest and serve at once.

——— ••• ———

Quail with Burghul, Mushrooms and Hazelnuts

The technique of poaching quails in milk is used by Arabella Boxer and Philippa Beck in *The Herb Book* published by Marks and Spencer. The initial cooking in milk seems to make the quails swell – quite useful with such small birds.

serves 4

For the burghul
1 small onion,
85 g (3 oz) unsalted butter
170 g (6 oz) coarse burghul,
    (cracked wheat)
2 shallots, finely chopped
120 g (4 oz) skinned hazelnuts,
    toasted and chopped
120 g (4 oz) mushrooms, chopped

120 g (4 oz) smoked ham, diced
6 tablespoons finely chopped parsley
salt and pepper

For the quail
8 quail
1 litre ($1\frac{3}{4}$ pints) milk
3 tablespoons melted butter
salt and pepper

Sauté the onion in a few tablespoons of the butter until soft. Add the burghul and stir to coat in the fat. Pour a good 300 ml ($\frac{1}{2}$ pint) of boiling water over the burghul, stir, add some salt and pepper, cover, and simmer gently for about 20 minutes. Meanwhile sauté the shallots in a few tablespoons of the butter until soft, add the mushrooms and cook over high heat until they start to take on colour. Season with salt and pepper. Stir in the hazelnuts, ham and parsley. When the burghul is tender turn it out into a shallow bowl. Toss with the rest of the butter and fold in the mushroom mixture.

Meanwhile place the quail in a large saucepan and cover with milk. Bring to the boil and simmer for 7 minutes. Drain them, pat dry and season with salt and pepper. Place the burghul in a shallow oven dish which can also be served from. Set the quail on top and brush with the melted butter. Roast in an oven preheated to 200°C/ 400°F/gas 6 for about 8 minutes, basting once with butter. Serve immediately.

Quail Stuffed with Wild Rice and Orange

serves 4

8 quail
1 large navel orange
1 carrot, finely chopped
2 shallots, finely chopped
3 oz (80 g) clarified butter
1 stick of celery, finely chopped
100 g (3½ oz) wild rice
1 tablespoon pine nuts

1 tablespoon currants
300 ml (½ pint) chicken stock
4 tablespoons brandy
1 teaspoon slaked arrowroot
  (optional)
caster sugar
salt and pepper

Peel the skin (without the pith) from the orange in strips. Cut the strips into julienne and blanch for 15 minutes in 1 litre (1¾ pints) of boiling water. Cut the flesh of the orange into segments and set aside.

Sweat the vegetables in 1–2 tablespoons of the butter until they are golden and soft.

Soak the wild rice in cold water for one hour. Simmer gently, covered, in 200 ml (scant ½ pint) of water for 15 minutes. Divide the rice between a small oven dish and a bowl. Mix 2 tablespoons of butter, the currants, pine nuts, 1 teaspoon of the blanched julienne, chopped, half the softened vegetables, salt and pepper into the rice in the bowl.

Season the quail inside, then stuff the cavities with this rice mixture and truss into a neat shape. Heat the rest of the butter in a roasting tin in an oven heated to 220°C/425°F/gas 7. Place the quail in the tin and baste with the butter. Spoon the rest of the vegetables around the birds. Roast in the oven for 20 minutes, baste at least twice during this time. If the vegetables become too brown add a little of the stock to the pan. Skim the fat from the tin and flame with the brandy. Remove the birds to a warm dish and keep warm. Deglaze the pan with the stock and boil down to concentrate the flavours. Strain, pressing down on the vegetables, into a small saucepan. Add the arrowroot, (if you are using it) the orange segments and julienne and bring back to the boil.

Heat the extra rice, covered, in the oven for 12 minutes.

Serve the quail with a little sauce spooned over them and decorate with the orange slices and a little of the extra rice.

Note: if you have the quail livers, sauté them very briefly and mix with the rice before stuffing the birds. If you are trying to cut down on butter substitute 2 petit suisse, quark or fromage frais for the butter used in the rice.

Roast Quail in Vine Leaves
with Grapes

Vine leaves help keep the quails moist and gently scent the meat. Not surprisingly the flavour goes particularly well with grapes

serves 4

8 quail
2 tablespoons clarified butter
1 shallot, finely chopped
4 chicken livers
1 teaspoon fresh sage leaves,
    chopped
32 white grapes, Italia if possible,
    peeled and pipped
8 vine leaves, blanched if packed
    in brine

4 slices green fatty streaky bacon
5 tablespoons armagnac
300 ml ($\frac{1}{2}$ pint) good game or
    chicken stock
1 tablespoon arrowroot
salt and freshly ground black
    pepper

Preheat the oven to 240°C/475°F/gas 9. Sauté the shallot in 1 tablespoon of butter and oil, stirring, until the shallot softens. Add the livers and sauté for a few minute until lightly cooked, but still pink inside. Scrap into a bowl and deglaze the pan with 1 tablespoon of the armagnac. Add this to the livers with several grapes and the sage. Chop the mixture coarsely, season, and use to stuff the quail. Wrap the birds in vine leaves and secure with a rasher of bacon. Heat the roasting pan on top of the stove with a tablespoon of clarified butter. Place the quail in the pan – they should fit nicely but not be too crowded. Roast for 15 minutes. Take the pan out of the oven and flame with 2 tablespoons of armagnac. Lower the oven to 190°C/375°F/gas 5 and roast for 10 minutes more. Set the birds on a warm serving dish and take off the bacon and vine leaves. Degrease the pan and deglaze with the remaining armagnac. Add the stock and simmer a minute or two before adding the remaining grapes and heating them through. Slake the arrowroot, stir into the sauce and simmer for

1 minute more. Taste for seasoning. Serve the birds with a few spoon-fuls of sauce and several grapes.

Quail in Lettuce with Kumquats

This is one of my favourite recipes for quail. You could serve it on small potato galettes if you wanted it to be more substantial. A good recipe for supermarket quail which come without the tasty livers and hearts.

serves 4

8 quail	300 ml ($\frac{1}{2}$ pint) good chicken stock
2 tablespoons oil	2 teaspoons brandy
120 g (4 oz) unsalted butter	2 teaspoons arrowroot
32 kumquats	salt and freshly ground black
50 g (2 oz) sugar	pepper
16 leaves of Batavia or other	
large-leafed lettuce	

Season the prepared birds and brown in the oil and 30 g (1 oz) of the butter. Peel the skin off 8 kumquats – easy to do with your fingers – and chop the skin coarsely. Mix the chopped skin with the remaining butter. Divide it into 8 knobs and stuff the cavities of the quail. Blanch the lettuce leaves by pouring boiling water over them and leaving for a minute or two. Dry on tea towels then cut out the thick centre stalks. Wrap each quail in 2 leaves and place in a flameproof casserole just large enough to contain the birds in one layer. Pour half the stock into the casserole. Bring the stock to a simmer before cover-ing and placing in a preheated oven 180°C/350°F/gas 4 for 20 minutes.

Meanwhile cut the rest of the kumquats into 4 segments and remove the pips. Place in a small saucepan with the sugar and 300 ml ($\frac{1}{2}$ pint) of water. Simmer for 10 minutes then drain. The syrup can be kept for fruit salads.

Remove the quail to a warmed serving dish. Pour the cooking juices into a saucepan, add the rest of the stock, the brandy, and the kumquats and bring to a simmer. Slake the arrowroot with a little cold water and stir into the pan. Simmer for a minute to thicken, adjust the seasoning and serve with the quail.

Quails in Peppers

serves 2

2 large yellow peppers	8 vine leaves
2 tablespoons extra virgin olive oil	4 quail
125 g (4 oz) pancetta, cut into matchsticks	salt and pepper

Cut the peppers in half horizontally, cutting through the stem and leaving it attached. Carefully remove the seeds without tearing the peppers. Place on a hot grill, skin side up and grill until the peppers are beginning to get brown blotches and become softer. Peel off the charred skin with wet fingers and set the peppers aside. Place the pancetta in a heavy frying pan and brown. Remove with a slotted spoon and drain on kitchen paper. Pour away all but 1 tablespoon of the fat in the pan, add the oil and brown the quails. Season them well with salt and pepper. Arrange some pancetta pieces in each half-pepper, place the quails on top and scatter over the remaining pancetta. Blanch the vine leaves if they are fresh, wash them under running water if they come out of a package. Tuck two leaves over each quail and place in an oiled roasting tin. Roast in an oven preheated to 200°C/400°F/gas 6 for 20 minutes.

Spatchcocked Quail with Mushrooms and Polenta

serves 6

6 quail
5 tablespoons olive oil
juice of one lemon
teaspoon each of chopped thyme, rosemary and oregano
knob of butter
1 clove garlic, crushed and finely chopped
450 g (1 lb) wild mushrooms or a mixture of cultivated ones such as oyster and brown-cap, sliced

1.25 litre (2 pints) chicken stock
200 g (7 oz) coarse polenta (cornmeal)
150 ml ($\frac{1}{4}$ pint) game or chicken stock
a handful of sultanas soaked in grappa or brandy (optional)
salt and freshly ground black pepper

Spatchcock the quails following the final recipe in this chapter, Roast Quail with Breadcrumbs and Herbs. Mix 4 tablespoons of the olive oil, lemon juice, and herbs with some salt and pepper, then rub this into the quails. Leave for at least one hour.

While the quails are marinating prepare the mushrooms and polenta. Heat the butter and remaining oil in a heavy frying pan; add the garlic and cook gently to soften without colouring. Stir in the mushrooms, salt and pepper and sauté until the mushrooms are cooked. Set aside. Bring the 1.25 litre (2 pints) of chicken stock to the boil, add the polenta in a slow steady stream, stir with a wooden spoon until the polenta is cooked and comes away from the sides of the pan, about 35 minutes. Heat the game stock in a small saucepan and add the sultanas. Ten minutes before the polenta is ready grill the birds. Place a small mound of polenta in each dish, make a well in the centre and fill with some mushrooms and a half quail. Pour some stock and sultanas around the edge.

Note: You can get away with one quail per person here because the polenta is so filling.

Quail Stuffed with Papaya and Lime

serves 6–8

8 quail

2 limes

2 ripe papayas

60 g (2 oz) unsalted butter

2 tablespoons olive oil

300 ml ($\frac{1}{2}$ pint) chicken stock

2 teaspoons arrowroot (optional)

salt and freshly ground black
   pepper

Remove the zest from the limes in strips with a potato peeler. Cut the strips into fine julienne and blanch in boiling water for 15 minutes. Refresh under cold running water, drain and set aside.

Cut the papayas in half, scoop out the seeds and discard them. Cut the halves into thin slices, then cut off the skin. Chop the flesh into small dice, place in a bowl and mix with the juice of one lime, salt and pepper.

Make a slit down the back of the quail and bone out the centre bones; leave the legs intact. This is not as hard as it sounds if you use a flexible knife and take short strokes along the side of the carcase. Lightly season the inside quail meat, place some papaya in the centre and sew up the quails. Use black thread so it will be easy to remove later. Tie the legs together to keep the shape neat. Heat the oil and a knob of butter in a sauté pan and brown the quails on all sides. Pour away the oil, add the stock and bring to a boil. Cover the quail with a round of greaseproof paper and a lid and simmer very gently until they are tender, about 25 minutes. Remove the birds to a heated dish. Boil the pan juices for a few minutes to thicken them slightly, then whisk in the remaining butter, bit by bit, on and off the heat so the butter thickens the sauce. Alternatively dissolve the arrowroot in 2 tablespoons of cold water, add to the stock and simmer for a few minutes. Adjust the seasoning and serve poured over the quail. Sprinkle the julienne of lime over the top and serve at once.

———— •●• ————

Quail with Saffron Rice

serves 4

a good pinch of saffron
2 tablespoons white wine
50 g (2 oz) goose fat or half lard
and half butter
170 g ham (6 oz), cut into small
lardons
4 shallots, very finely chopped

8 quail
700 ml (1¾ pints) good chicken
stock
270 g (9½ oz) long grain rice
1 tablespoon finely chopped
parsley
salt and pepper

Place the saffron in the wine and leave to infuse. Using a flame-proof casserole large enough to hold the birds in one layer, heat the fat and brown the shallots, ham and quails. When the quails are golden on all sides (about 8 minutes) remove them from the casserole to a plate and cover loosely with foil to keep warm. Add the stock to the casserole and bring to the boil. Place the rice in a sieve and wash under running water, then drain the rice and add it to the boiling stock. Add the saffron and infused wine and the bouquet garni and stir just until the stock returns to the boil. Cover the casserole and do not stir again. Either continue cooking the rice over a very low heat or place the casserole in a preheated oven 170°C/325°F/gas 3. After 10 minutes add the quail to the casserole, carefully placing them on top of the rice without disturbing the bottom layer of rice. Cover and continue to cook for about 15 minutes, or until the rice has absorbed all the liquid. Remove the quails to a hot dish. Fluff up the rice with a fork and serve either around the quail or in a separate dish, decorated with parsley.

———— •●• ————

Stuffed Roast Quails with
a Red Wine Sauce

If you have time bone out the breasts following the instructions for Boned Pheasant Perigord (Chapter 3) but only removing the carcase and leaving the legs intact. This is quite quick to do as boning legs is the fiddly bit.

serves 6

For the stuffing
2 tablespoons butter
140 g (5 oz) mushrooms, finely
  chopped
squeeze of lemon juice
200 g (7 oz) green streaky bacon,
  chopped
200 g (7 oz) lean minced pork
12 quail livers
1 tablespoon bread crumbs
1 tablespoon cognac
$\frac{1}{2}$ tablespoon very finely chopped
  parsley
salt and pepper
12 quail, boned if possible
melted butter

For the sauce
1 tablespoon oil
2 shallots, very finely chopped
1 half carrot, very finely chopped
$\frac{1}{2}$ stick celery, very finely chopped
$\frac{1}{2}$ bottle decent red wine
300 ml ($\frac{1}{2}$ pint) brown chicken
  stock
25 g (1 oz) unsalted butter
salt and pepper
12 white bread croûtes, fried until
  golden in butter

Sauté the mushrooms in half the butter, stirring, until they give off their juices. Season with lemon juice, salt and pepper and boil hard until the mushrooms are nearly dry. Scrape into a bowl. Add the remaining butter to the pan and sauté the bacon, pork, and livers until lightly cooked. Pour away most of the fat and add the meat to the mushrooms. Stir in the breadcrumbs, cognac and parsley and season well.

Stuff the birds with the mixture, sew them up with black thread, if boned, and truss them into a neat shape. Season lightly and place in a buttered roasting pan. Paint the birds with melted butter and roast in an oven preheated to 230°C/450°F/gas 8 for 15 minutes.

Meanwhile sauté the carrots for a minute of two in the oil before adding the shallots and celery. Continue to sauté, stirring until the vegetables soften and are lightly coloured. Deglaze with the wine and reduce by half. Add the stock and reduce slightly. Strain into a clean pan, pressing down on the vegetables to extract all the flavour. When the quails are cooked remove them to a hot dish, degrease the roasting pan and deglaze with a few tablespoons of sauce. Combine this with the rest of the sauce. Bring the sauce to a simmer, swirl in the butter gradually, on and off the heat to thicken the sauce. Taste for seasoning. Arrange the quail on the hot crisp croûtes and coat with the sauce.

Quail with Raisins

If you have a bit of stock to braise the quail in so much the better but water will do as the bacon and cognac used in the recipe will provide enough flavour.

serves 8

100 g ($3\frac{1}{2}$ oz) stoned raisins
3 petit suisse or 4–5 tablespoons of
  fromage frais
2 tablespoons butter
2 tablespoons oil
8 quail
200 g (7 oz) unsmoked pancetta or
  green thick streaky bacon
  rashers

3 tablespoons cognac
150 ml ($\frac{1}{4}$ pint) of chicken stock or
  water
1 tablespoon cream
salt and freshly ground black
  pepper

Cover the raisins with warm tea and leave for a few hours or overnight. Mix the petit suisse with about 2 tablespoons of the raisins and season with salt and pepper. Stuff the quail with this mixture, truss them and season the outside skin. Heat the butter and oil in a sauté pan and brown the quail on all sides. Remove them from the pan. Cut the bacon into lardons and brown in the pan. Pour away all the fat, return the birds to the pan and add the drained raisins. Pour the cognac over the birds and reduce by half. Add the stock or water, cover with a sheet of greaseproof paper and a lid and simmer gently on top of the stove for about 20–25 minutes, turning the quails halfway through the cooking time. Place the quails on a warm dish and keep warm. Simmer the cooking juices, scraping up bits from the bottom of the pan. Add the cream, adjust the seasoning and pour over the birds and serve.

Quail with Apple

serves 4

8 quail	4 firm Cox's orange pippins
2 tablespoons oil	juice from $\frac{1}{2}$ lemon
6 tablespoons butter	1 tablespoon icing sugar
6 tablespoons madeira	8 croûtes, fried in butter
250 ml (scant $\frac{1}{2}$ pint) chicken stock	salt and freshly ground black pepper

Season the quail inside and out and truss. Heat the oil and butter in a sauté pan and brown the quail on all sides. This should take about 3-4 minutes. Remove the birds from the pan and pour away the fat. Add the madeira and boil hard until it has reduced to 2 tablespoons. Pour in the stock and bring to a simmer. Return the quail to the pan, cover with a sheet of greaseproof paper and a lid and simmer gently for about 20–25 minutes.

Meanwhile peel, core and cut the apples into slices. Toss them in the lemon juice as they are prepared, to prevent discolouration. Heat a small frying pan with 2 tablespoons of butter. Dry the apple slices and when the butter is very hot sauté the slices quickly, add the sugar and some pepper and continue to sauté until the apples are lightly browned and lightly cooked. Keep them warm until serving.

When the quails are cooked arrange them on the hot croûtes. Quickly reduce the cooking juices for a minute or two. Taste for seasoning and swirl in the remaining 2 tablespoons of butter so it thickens the sauce rather than melts into it. Coat the birds with the sauce and decorate with the apple slices.

Variation: Quince is delicious with quail and can replace the apple in this recipe. Wash, core and slice 2 quinces without peeling them. Fry them gently in butter in a covered pan until they soften. Uncover the pan, add the sugar and allow them to colour slightly. Serve with the quail as in the above recipe.

——— •●• ———

Quail with Fruit

serves 4

8 slices of bread	2 eating apples
clarified butter	1 teaspoon sugar
8 cooked prunes	2 tablespoons cream
150 ml ($\frac{1}{4}$ pint) armagnac	salt and pepper
150 ml ($\frac{1}{4}$ pint) chicken stock	

Cut 8 ovals large enough for the quails to sit on from the bread. Fry in butter, drain on kitchen paper and keep warm. Season the insides of the birds and stuff each one with a prune. Heat a good knob of butter in a frying pan and brown the birds on all sides. Arrange them in a casserole. Heat the armagnac, pour over the birds and flame. Add the hot chicken stock, cover with a sheet of greaseproof paper and a lid and place in an oven preheated to 180°C/350°F/gas 4 for 30 minutes.

Meanwhile core, peel and cut 8 rounds from the apples. Fry these in butter until soft, add the sugar and caramelise the slices. Keep warm.

When the quails are cooked set them on the fried bread on a round of apple. Add the cream to the cooking juices, boil for a minute or two, adjust the seasoning and spoon over the quail.

——— •●• ———

Smoked Quail

This unusual recipe is from the exceptionally attractive cookbook *Chinese Delights* by Lisa Kinsman with photographs by Christine Hanscomb (1982).

serves 4

4 quail	1 clove crushed garlic
2 tablespoons groundnut oil	1 tablespoon cooking wine or sherry

For the marinade

To smoke

1 tablespoons honey
2 tablespoons China tea
3 tablespoons dark soy sauce
1 tablespoon sweet chilli sauce or

For the decoration

tomato sauce
4–6 spring onions carved into
2 cloves star anise
flowers
$\frac{1}{2}$ teaspoon five-spice powder
watercress

To make the spring-onion flowers, cut off the root then cut off the green part leaving a whole spring onion 7.5 cm (5 inches) long. Criss-cross both ends with a sharp knife leaving 2.5 cm (1 inch) uncut in the centre. Submerge in iced water and the ends will curl outwards. Keep in cold water until required.

Skin and clean the quail. Mix marinade ingredients, rub over quail and leave in a bowl for 2–3 hours.

Preheat the oven to 200°C/400°F/gas 6. Heat the oil in a wok or frying pan for 1–2 minutes until it starts to smoke, cook the quail for 7–10 minutes on all sides particularly over the breast where the meat is thicker. Turn the heat lower if the quails start to burn. Remove to a roasting tin, place in the centre of the oven and roast for 10 minutes.

Put the tea leaves in a clean wok or large saucepan. Place a wire rack over them and cover. Turn the heat to high for about 1 minute or until the tea starts to smoke. Quickly remove the lid and place the quail on the rack, replace the lid and smoke for approximately 30 seconds. Serve on a heated dish decorated with the spring-onion flowers and watercress.

Cold Quail with Tarragon Jelly

serves 6

6 good-sized quail
7 sprigs of tarragon
salt and pepper
3 tablespoons madeira

4 tablespoons clarified unsalted
   butter
550 ml (1 pint) jellied chicken stock

Season the inside of each quail with salt and pepper and a sprig of tarragon. Truss them neatly and place in a low casserole just large enough for the birds. Place in a preheated oven 230°C/450°F/gas 8 for 10 minutes. Drain off all the fat. Pour the madeira over the quails, then add the hot stock and the leaves from the last sprig of tarragon. Cover and simmer slowly for 12 minutes, either in the oven or on top of the stove. When the quails are cooked remove them to a large gratin dish or large shallow bowl. Degrease the stock thoroughly. Use kitchen paper to blot up any last bits of fat on the surface and pour the stock over around the quail. Place in the refrigerator and serve when the jelly has set.

Note: The stock can also be poured into a low tray to set, then cut into dice and placed around the quail. If the tray is first lined with cling-film the jelly can be turned out and the cling-film peeled off before the jelly is chopped.

———— •●• ————

Roast Quail with Breadcrumbs and Herbs

serves 4

8 quail
120 g (4 oz) fresh breadcrumbs
3 tablespoons parsley, chopped
   very fine
1 tablespoon chervil or tarragon
   chopped very fine

1 tablespoon chives chopped very
   fine
85 g (3 oz) unsalted butter
salt and freshly ground black
   pepper

Using kitchen scissors, cut along one side of the backbone from the tail to the neck. Open out the bird and lay it on a flat surface breast-upward. Press down on the breast with the palm of your hand to flatten the bird. Make a small slit in the bottom flap of skin and ease the legs through to keep the bird in a tight neat shape. Mix the breadcrumbs with the herbs and season with salt and pepper. Melt the butter and pour into a shallow dish. Season the quails and soak in the butter, then dip into the breadcrumbs. Place the birds in a lightly oiled roasting tin and roast in a preheated oven 200°C/400°F/gas 6 for 15 minutes. Baste with butter half way through the cooking time. The birds can be prepared in advance but should be roasted just before serving.

RABBIT
AND HARE

Rabbit

ORIGINALLY the European rabbit inhabited the western end of the Mediterranean in southern France and Iberia, but it has been spread, by man, throughout most of Europe and to other continents. It is not certain when rabbits came to Britain but by the late twelfth century they were semi-domesticated and raised in long man-made burrows or conygers and were part of the livestock of many manor houses. Later, rabbits escaped and thrived on the grasses of temperate Britain. Their population continued to increase over the centuries until in the early 1950s recurrent epidemics of myxamatosis reduced their numbers.

Today wild rabbits are back in force, at least in Gloucestershire, where we count dozens scurrying across our rough deep lane and many more running across the field at the sound of the car. Some degree of immunity seems to be establishing itself. Before the 1950s rabbits were plentiful and inexpensive. Many unemployed families in the 'hungry thirties' were kept alive by them and a good shot could bag 30 an hour. They are also ferreted. Our son sent off for ferrets to the same place in Cambridgeshire where we later discovered my Irish father, then in his eighties, had got his ferrets when he was a boy.

A young rabbit, which makes the best eating, should have soft ears which can be easily torn, and sharp teeth and claws. Wild and hutch rabbits belong to the same species but there is a great difference in size and flavour. The smaller wild rabbit has darker and stronger tasting flesh than that of the domesticated hutch rabbit. There is open season for wild rabbits and with the decline of myxamatosis they should be easy to obtain from game dealers. The hutch rabbit, too, is more readily available fresh, and deserves to be very popular for its delicate flavour. They are best between $3-3\frac{1}{2}$ months old when plump, with a good bit of white fat round the kidneys and a bright red liver. Supermarkets sell very acceptable fresh rabbit joints but without any offal. Wild rabbit can be soaked overnight in acidulated water for a milder taste. It will also need slightly longer cooking times than the domesticated rabbit. All the recipes included here have been made with hutch rabbit – my preference.

A rabbit is skinned in much the same manner as a hare. See below.

OF THE TWO types of hare commonly eaten in Britain, the brown hare is the larger and more tender. Its back or saddle is generally roasted and the legs and shoulders braised. The smaller mountain hare, sometimes called the blue hare in Scotland, weighs between 2–2.4 kg (5–6 lbs), because its flavour is inferior it should be kept for civets or stews. A young hare, up to a year old, is called a leveret and can be identified by its tender ears, smooth coat and small, sharp white teeth. An older hare will have thick, tough ears and long, yellow teeth.

Hares need to be hung, head down, and undrawn, for between 3–5 days or longer if the animal is large and the weather cold. When the hare is drawn, the blood, particularly that trapped in the chest cavity, should be saved as a sauce thickener. A few drops of vinegar added to the blood will prevent coagulation. Hares, particularly older animals, benefit from marinades. The meat is lean and any roast will need basting or larding.

To skin a hare hang it on a hook by its back paws. Make a circular incision in the skin above the first joint. Cut down the back of each hind leg and pull the skin off. Cut through the skin below the tail and the vent, and peel back the skin gently, turning it inside out and leaving the tail attached to the body. Pull the skin down over the body and forelegs and sever the skin at the base of each foreleg. Peel the skin from the neck and over the head as far as the ears. Cut off the ears at the base. Cut the skin free round the eyes and mouth and pull the skin right off the muzzle. Lift the flesh of the belly to avoid piercing the intestines before making a slit up the middle of the belly to draw out all the innards. Reserve the liver and kidneys. Place a tablespoon of vinegar in a bowl, slit the diaphragm open at the base of the chest with a sharp knife and catch the released blood in the bowl. Rinse the hare in cold water, dry, and remove the blue membrane.

———— •●• ————

Rabbit with Mustard

A classic dish, easy to prepare and very tasty to eat. It is traditionally served with pasta.

serves 5–6

1.5 kg (3 lb) rabbit pieces
3 tablespoons prepared Dijon
  mustard
1 tablespoon oil
150 ml ($\frac{1}{4}$ pint) chicken stock

2 tablespoons vermouth or dry
  white wine
6 tablespoons crème fraîche or
  double cream

Mix the mustard with the oil and season with salt and pepper. Spread the mustard mixture over the lightly seasoned rabbit pieces and place them in one layer in a roasting tin. Bake in an oven preheated to 220°C/425°F/gas 7 for 5 minutes. Pour the stock over the rabbit and continue to roast for another 20 minutes, basting a few times during the cooking time. Remove the rabbit to a warm serving dish. Degrease the roasting tin before deglazing with the wine. Stir in the cream and simmer for a few minutes. Season and strain over the rabbit. Serve immediately.

Wild Rabbit with Tarragon

serves 6

1 onion, chopped
1 stalk of celery, chopped
1 carrot, finely chopped
1 leek, chopped
1 clove garlic, crushed
bouquet garni
2 young wild rabbits, jointed
seasoned flour

groundnut oil
600 ml (1 pint) dry white wine
4 tablespoons cream
$1\frac{1}{2}$ tablespoons fresh chopped
  tarragon leaves
2 teaspoons Dijon mustard
salt and freshly ground black
  pepper

Heat a few tablespoons of oil in a heavy sauté pan, add all the vegetables except the garlic and stir until they are somewhat softened. Stir in the garlic and cook for another minute or two. Remove the vegetables with a slotted spoon to a casserole. Lightly flour the rabbit

111

pieces, add a bit more oil to the pan and sauté the rabbit until lightly coloured. Add the rabbit to the casserole, tip out any oil in the pan and deglaze with some of the white wine. Pour this into the casserole along with the rest of the wine. Tuck the bouquet garni among the rabbit pieces, cover the casserole with a sheet of greaseproof paper and a lid. Bring to the boil on top of the stove before simmering gently in an oven preheated to 150°C/300°F/gas 3 for about 30 minutes.

Meanwhile mix one tablespoon of the tarragon into the cream and leave to infuse. When the rabbit is cooked remove the pieces to a heated dish. Sieve the sauce into a saucepan pressing on all the vegetables to extract the flavour. Bring to a simmer, add the mustard and cream and simmer until the flavours have blended. Adjust the seasoning and pour over the rabbit. Decorate with the remaining tarragon.

Note: The vegetables can be kept and served with the rabbit rather than strained into the sauce.

Grilled or Roasted Rabbit Marinated in Olive Oil and Herbs

serves 6

1.50 kg (3½ lbs) rabbit pieces	3 cloves garlic, crushed and chopped
150 ml (¼ pint) olive oil	2 shallots, chopped
1 tablespoon dried thyme	glass of red or white wine
½ tablespoon dried oregano	salt and freshly ground black
½ tablespoon dried rosemary	pepper

Mix all the ingredients together and marinate the rabbit in the mixture for 24 hours in a cool place. Grill the rabbit over charcoal or roast in the top of an oven preheated to 250°C/500°F/gas 10 until the meat is cooked through and brown on the outside. Serve with salad, olives, and new potatoes.

Variation: Use a marinade made with 2 teaspoons of fresh grated ginger, grated zest and juice from 2 limes, 2 tablespoons soy sauce, 2 tablespoons sesame oil, 4 tablespoons groundnut oil and 1 clove of chopped garlic.

Gibelotte de Lapereau

A recipe from the chef de cuisine, Christian Guillut, of the Ecole de Gastronomie Française Ritz-Escoffier. I attended some trial classes of this new school located in the cellars of the Ritz hotel in Paris. This rabbit stew was on our menu and we jointed and braised the rabbit under the chef's surveillance. The small pieces of rabbit and pork which were not designated for the stew were whisked away to a back burner and simmered for most of the day to provide a *rillette* for the chef. The livers disappeared into the Ritz kitchens to keep the big chefs happy there. The pleasure our chef had in watching over his little *rillette* cooking was a delight to witness.

serves 4

2 tablespoon oil	500 ml (scant pint) veal stock
200 g (7 oz) salt pork (belly), thick slices cut into lardons	bouquet garni
	3 shallots, finely chopped
75 g (3 oz) unsalted butter	1 clove garlic, crushed
200 g (7 oz) pickling onions, skinned	salt and pepper
	200 g (7 oz) button mushrooms, cleaned
1 rabbit weighing 1 kg 250 g (2 lb 12 oz) cut into 8 pieces	some very finely chopped parsley to decorate
1½ tablespoons flour	
250 ml (scant half pint) white wine	

Heat the oil in a large sauteuse and brown the lardons. Remove them from the pan, add 50 g (2 oz) of the butter and when it is hot lightly brown the onions. Remove them from the pan. Pat the rabbit pieces dry, remove any fragments of bone, season, and place them in the hot fat to brown. When both sides are nicely coloured sift the flour over the meat and cook for a further few minutes, turning the rabbit to distribute the flour. Pour off the fat and add the wine. Reduce the wine by half before adding the stock, bouquet garni, shallots, garlic, onions and lardons. Place a sheet of greaseproof paper over the rabbit before covering with a lid. Simmer gently on top of the stove for 35 minutes. Before the rabbit has finished cooking sauté the mushrooms in the remaining butter and season. Before serving lift the pieces of rabbit on to a serving bowl. Remove the bouquet garni and taste the sauce for seasoning. Pour the sauce and vegetables over the rabbit, add the mushrooms and sprinkle the parsley on top. Serve piping hot.

Note: Italian pancetta is the nearest equivalent to the French belly of pork. Chicken stock can be substituted for the veal stock.

Rabbit with Apricots

serves 4

1.8 kg (4 lb) rabbit pieces
230 g (8 oz) dried apricot halves

For the marinade
2 onions
1 shallot
1 carrot
a few stalks of parsley
1 bottle dry white wine
25 g (1 oz) butter
2 tablespoons olive oil

1 carrot, very finely diced
2 shallots very finely chopped
$\frac{1}{2}$ stalk celery, very finely chopped
1 clove garlic, very finely chopped
2 tablespoons flour
2 heaped tablespoons of low-sugar apricot jam
bouquet garni
chicken stock
salt and freshly ground black pepper

Soak the apricots overnight in enough boiling water to cover. Marinate the rabbit in the marinade ingredients for 24 hours. Remove the rabbit from the marinade and dry. Bring the marinade to a boil, skim, then strain and set aside.

Heat the oil and butter in a frying pan, season the rabbit and brown on all sides. Remove the rabbit from the pan and add the chopped vegetables. Stir them until they become soft, then stir in the flour and cook a few minutes more. Deglaze the pan with some of the strained marinade. Pour the contents of the pan into a flameproof casserole. Stir in 2 tablespoons of the jam and place the meat on top. Add the rest of the marinade and the bouquet garni. Cover with stock. Bring to the boil, cover with a sheet of greaseproof paper and a lid. Place in an oven heated to 170°C/325°F/gas 3 for 40 minutes. Heat the apricots in a small saucepan. Remove the rabbit to a hot serving dish. Strain the sauce, pressing well to extract as much juice as possible, season to taste and add the rest of the jam if needed. Pour over the rabbit and garnish with the reserved apricots.

Rabbit with Cider

serves 4

1 rabbit, cut into serving portions
  or if possible 1.25 kg (2½ lbs) of
  rabbit pieces
1 bottle of dry cider, French if
  possible
45 g (1½ oz) unsalted butter

a little oil
8 shallots, peeled
2 tablespoons redcurrant jelly
2 tablespoons flour
bouquet garni
salt and freshly ground black pepper

Pat the pieces of rabbit dry and season with salt and pepper. Heat the butter with a bit of oil in a large sauteuse and brown the rabbit on both sides. Remove the rabbit from the pan and brown the shallots. Return the rabbit to the pan and sift the flour evenly over the top. Stir over moderate heat to cook the flour and distribute it evenly. Add the bouquet garni, salt and pepper and the cider. When it comes to the boil, cover with a sheet of greaseproof paper and a lid and simmer gently for 25–30 minutes. Lift the rabbit onto a warm serving plate and keep warm in a low oven. Discard the bouquet garni, stir the redcurrant jelly into the cooking juices and adjust the seasoning. Spoon the sauce over the rabbit and serve.

Rabbit with Prunes

serves 4

20 prunes
cup of china tea
1 rabbit cut into pieces
2 tablespoons oil
1 tablespoon butter
3 carrots, cut into small dice
4 shallots, finely chopped

4 tablespoons dry vermouth
300 ml (½ pint) good chicken stock
bouquet garni, with 2 sprigs of thyme
  included
salt and freshly ground black pepper
fresh thyme, finely chopped, to
  decorate

Soak the prunes in the tea overnight or heat them gently together until the prunes soften.

    Dry, season and brown the rabbit pieces in the mixture of oil and butter. Place them in a casserole and add the carrots to the pan. Stir until they begin to colour them lower the heat and add the shallots. Keep stirring until the shallots soften, then pour in the vermouth and

115

reduce by half, scraping up any brown bits from the pan at the same time. Add this to the casserole along with the stock, prunes and bouquet garni. Bring to a simmer on top of the stove before placing in a preheated oven at 150°C/300°F/gas 2 for about 1 hour or until the rabbit is cooked. Remove the bouquet garni. Strain off the cooking juices (leaving the vegetables behind) and reduce in a saucepan to concentrate the flavour. Season and pour back over the rabbit, vegetables and prunes. Decorate with a few chopped fresh thyme leaves if available.

The Wanderer's Rabbit

These two excellent and up-to-date recipes come from a charming very small book, '*Dressed Game and Poultry à la Mode*' by Mrs De Salis, published in 1888. In her preface she states that she has consulted all the known and unknown tomes on the gourmet's art and preserved such recipes that from her own personal experience she knows to be good.

Recipe I

Divide a rabbit into pieces of convenient size, put them into a saucepan in which half a dozen slices of bacon are cooking. As soon as the meat is beginning to brown, pour a wineglass and a half of brandy into the saucepan, and set fire to it. When the fire has burnt out, add a little pepper, salt, a bay leaf, and a bit of thyme, and let it simmer by the side of the fire till the brandy has nearly dried up, then serve.

Recipe II

Divide a couple of rabbits into quarters, adding plenty of pepper and salt. Slightly fry them in a saucepan in bacon fat and flour. Add sufficient stock and two glasses of sauternes, and let it stew on a moderate fire. When done, squeeze an orange over the dish just before serving up.

Stuffed Saddle of Rabbit

serves 4

2 saddles of rabbit plus livers and
   kidneys
4 tablespoons ground nut oil
150 ml ($\frac{1}{4}$ pint) dry white wine
1 shallot, chopped
half a carrot, finely chopped
bouquet garni

a large piece of caul fat
3 tablespoons bread crumbs
1 tablespoon melted butter
2 teaspoons finely chopped parsley
45 g ($1\frac{1}{2}$ oz) butter, chilled and
   diced
salt and pepper

Slice the kidneys and livers, cut into dice and season lightly. Heat half the oil in a frying pan and quickly seal the kidney and liver. Remove from the pan and set aside. Carefully bone the saddles. Chop the bones, add them to the frying pan with the carrot and shallot and the rest of the oil. Sauté over brisk heat, stirring occasionally, until the bones and vegetables are brown. Pour in the wine and reduce by half, then add the bouquet garni and 300 ml ($\frac{1}{2}$ pint) of water. Simmer, partially covered for 1 hour. Strain through a fine sieve, degrease and set aside.

Wash the caul in hot water to make it more supple, and spread it out on a flat surface. Cut into two large rectangles. Add the bread-crumbs, melted butter and parsley to the liver mixture and season well. Season the saddles and divide the stuffing between them and roll up into cylinders. Wrap each cylinder in caul. Roast the saddles in an oven preheated to 200°C/400°F/gas 6 for 15 minutes. Place on a hot serving dish and cover loosely with foil while you finish off the sauce. Pour off any fat from the roasting tin, deglaze with the stock. Continue to boil hard until it is reduced by half. Whisk in the butter, a few pieces at a time, on and off the heat so the butter thickens the sauce rather then melts in it. To serve, place some sauce on the plates and set a few slices of the stuffed saddle on top.

Note: The rest of the rabbits can go for compôte or any of the stews

——— •●• ———

Rabbit Casserole with Tomatoes

serves 4–5

1.25–1.50 kg (2½–3 lb) rabbit pieces
4 cloves garlic
300 ml (½ pint) dry white wine
2 tablespoons olive oil
1 onion, chopped
1 green pepper, chopped
450 ml (¾ pint) chopped tomatoes,
   canned or fresh

bouquet garni
½ dried chilli pepper
1 tablespoon tarragon wine vinegar
2 tablespoons finely chopped
   parsley
salt and freshly ground pepper

Skin the garlic cloves, cut one clove in half and rub the rabbit with it. Chop the other cloves, mix with the wine and use to marinate the rabbit for one to two hours. Remove the rabbit from the marinade, dry and season. Heat the oil in a frying pan and brown the rabbit pieces in a few batches. Remove them to a flameproof casserole. Add the onion and pepper to the frying pan and stir for a minute or two before adding the tomatoes, bouquet garni, chilli pepper and vinegar. Pour the vegetables over the rabbit, add the marinade and season with salt and pepper. Bring the casserole to a simmer before covering and simmering gently for 30 minutes. Discard the bouquet garni, adjust the seasoning and serve decorated with chopped parsley.

Smothered Rabbit

A homely stew that was popular in Hanoverian England.

serves 4

1 rabbit, cut into convenient-sized
   pieces
580 g (1¼ lb) onions,
2 cloves
1 bay leaf
a few peppercorns
230 g (8 oz) piece of salted pork
   belly or streaky bacon, cut into
   lardons

40 g (1½ oz) unsalted butter
1 tablespoon flour
150 ml (¼ pint) double cream
grated nutmeg
salt and pepper

Lightly brown the pork belly in a frying pan. Place it in a casserole and cover with the seasoned rabbit pieces, one onion, quartered, cloves, bay leaf and a few peppercorns. Cover with water and bring to a simmer, skim, and either simmer in a low oven or on top of the stove, covered, for about 1 hour. Strain the liquid (and spices and onion) into a saucepan and boil to reduce to about 250 ml (scant half pint).

Slice the rest of the onions and sweat them in the butter using a large frying pan. Stew them half covered until cooked and very soft. Stir in the flour then add the cream and rabbit stock, simmer for a minute or two to thicken, season well with salt, pepper and a few gratings of nutmeg. Pour over the rabbit, reheat if necessary and serve.

———— •••• ————

Jugged Hare

'Jugged' describes the container the hare cooks in and a large brown stoneware milk jug admirably suits the job although an ordinary casserole can also be used. It is a fruity dish and should be served with a salad and fruit to follow.

serves 6 or more

a hare, jointed, with liver and
    blood
seasoned flour
230 g (8 oz) piece of streaky bacon,
    cubed
230 g (8 oz) pickling onions
30 g (1 oz) lard
bouquet garni
300 ml ($\frac{1}{2}$ pint) beef stock
glass of port
1 tablespoon redcurrant jelly
salt and pepper

For the forcemeat balls
120 g (4 oz) fresh white
    breadcrumbs
60 g (2 oz) melted butter
1 tablespoon finely chopped
    parsley
$\frac{1}{2}$ tablespoon fresh thyme, finely
    chopped
1 egg, beaten
salt and pepper
lard for frying

Roll the hare in the seasoned flour. Heat the lard in a large frying pan and brown the hare, bacon and onions. As the pieces brown remove them to a jug or casserole. Pour off the fat from the frying pan and deglaze with the stock. Add to the jug along with the bouquet garni. Cover tightly with foil and stand in a deep saucepan of hot water. Place in an oven preheated to 150°C/300°F/gas 2 and cook for about 2 hours, or until the meat is very tender. Just before serving mash the liver in a little of the hot liquid and cook in a small saucepan for 5 minutes, stirring. Add the blood off the heat, then stir into the jug of hare. Meanwhile dissolve the redcurrant jelly in the port over low heat, stir it into the hare and season. Heat very gently, keeping it under boiling point, or the blood will separate, until the sauce thickens. Serve with forcemeat balls made by mixing the ingredients together, forming into balls, and frying in lard until golden brown

—— •••• ——

Hare with Smetana

serves 6

For the marinade
300 ml ($\frac{1}{2}$ pint) red wine
4 tablespoons red wine vinegar
1 onion, sliced
1 clove garlic, crushed
1 teaspoon each of dry mustard,
  salt, and sugar

5-6 juniper berries, crushed
$\frac{1}{2}$ bay leaf
1 young hare, jointed
30 g (1 oz) clarified butter
300 ml ($\frac{1}{2}$ pint) smetana, or soured
  cream

Marinate the hare for 2 days in the marinade. Remove the hare and strain the marinade into a saucepan. Reduce to half the quantity. Dry the hare joints and brown in the hot butter. Place the joints in a casserole, pour over the reduced marinade and the smetana. Cover and simmer in an oven preheated to 180°C/350°F/gas 4 for $1\frac{1}{2}$–2 hours.

Boned Saddle of Hare

serves 4

2 saddles of hare, boned, and
  bones reserved and chopped
7 tablespoons groundnut oil
1 large onion
1 carrot, chopped
1 stalk of celery, chopped
1 clove garlic, crushed
2 sprigs of thyme
1 bay leaf

6 juniper berries, crushed
8 peppercorns, crushed
450 ml ($\frac{3}{4}$ pint) red wine
150 ml ($\frac{1}{4}$ pint) beef stock
4 tablespoons double cream
2 tablespoons cognac
olive oil
butter
salt and pepper

Heat the groundnut oil in a roasting pan until it is nearly smoking. Add the bones and sear them for about 10 minutes, until they are brown but not charred. Add the vegetables, garlic, juniper berries and peppercorns and cook until they begin to colour. Place the tin in a hot oven, 220°C/425°F/gas 7, for about 20 minutes to colour the bones and vegetables even further. Be careful not to char the bones or they will give a bitter flavour to the sauce. Remove the pan from the oven, pour off the fat and discard. Add the wine and boil to reduce by half. Add 300 ml (1 pint) of water, and the stock, bring to the boil, and simmer for 30 minutes, skimming if necessary. Strain the sauce into a clean pan, stir in the cream and cognac and reduce until the sauce thickens slightly. Adjust the seasoning and set aside. Carefully remove and discard the thin membrane that covers the saddle. Season with salt and pepper and seal quickly in a few tablespoons of hot oil. Place the saddles in a roasting tin, smear with some butter and roast in a hot oven 200°C/400°F/gas 6 for 15 minutes. Place on a heated dish, cover loosely with foil and allow to rest for 5–10 minutes before carving.

Finish off the sauce by pouring away the fat from the roasting pan and deglazing with a little of the prepared sauce. Add this to the remaining stock, reheat and serve with thick slices of the hare.

Roast Saddle of Hare with Caramelised Apples

serves

2 saddles of hare

For the marinade:
1 carrot, finely chopped
one small onion, finely chopped
2 shallots, finely chopped
2 cloves garlic, crushed and
   chopped
3 strips of lemon peel
1 bay leaf
1 sprig of thyme
a few peppercorns and juniper
   berries, crushed

6 tablespoons olive oil
3 Cox's orange pippins
2 tablespoons olive oil
butter
1 tablespoon sugar
6 tablespoons white wine
8 tablespoons good game stock
1 tablespoon calvados
250 ml (scant $\frac{1}{2}$ pint) crème
   fraîche
salt and freshly ground black
   pepper

Place the saddles in an oval dish, add the marinade ingredients, turn the saddles in the mixture, cover tightly with cling-film and refrigerate for at least 24 hours. Turn the meat several times during this time.

Remove the saddles from the marinade, dry them and brown them in 2 tablespoons of hot olive oil in a roasting pan. Ease the fillets away from the chine bone with a sharp knife, without removing them, to make carving easier. Scoop out the marinade vegetables and place them in the pan, set the saddles on top and roast in a hot oven, 220°C/425°F/gas 7, for about 12 minutes.

Meanwhile prepare the apples by peeling, quartering, coring and slicing them. Heat a good knob of butter in a frying pan, add the apples and sauté gently until they are nearly tender. Raise the heat, add the sugar and caramelise the apples. Keep them warm over hot water or in a cool oven.

Remove the saddles to a heated dish and cover lightly with foil while you make the sauce. Degrease the pan, add the wine and boil hard until it evaporates. Add the stock, calvados and cream and continue to boil until the sauce has thickened slightly. Strain into a clean saucepan, season, and stir in about 30 g (1 oz) of cold butter. Do this last operation off and on the heat so the butter doesn't become oily and thin the sauce rather than thicken it. Remove the meat from the bones, carve into thick slices and serve with some sauce and apple slices.

Civet of Hare

serves 6

1 hare, jointed, with the blood

For the marinade
4 tablespoons brandy
2 shallots, sliced
1 clove garlic, crushed
2 sprigs of thyme
bay leaf

For the sauce
1 tablespoon oil
250 g ($\frac{1}{2}$ lb) piece of pancetta or, failing this, green streaky bacon, cut into lardons

1 onion, chopped
3 level tablespoons flour
450 ml ($\frac{3}{4}$ pints) red wine
$\frac{1}{2}$ teaspoon allspice
300 ml ($\frac{1}{2}$ pint) stock
24 pickling onions
45 g ($1\frac{1}{2}$ oz) unsalted butter
250 g (8 oz) mushrooms, sliced
2 tablespoons cream
6 pieces of fried bread
finely chopped parsley to decorate
salt and pepper

Combine the marinade ingredients together in a large bowl. Add the joints of hare, turning them in the marinade. Cover and refrigerate for 24–48 hours, turning the meat in the marinade several times.

Fry the lardons of pancetta until golden in a frying pan. Remove them to a casserole. Add the chopped onion and cook until it begins to colour, remove to the casserole. Drain the pieces of hare, reserving the marinade, and dry. Brown the hare in batches, adding the pieces

123

to the casserole when they are done. Sprinkle in the flour and allow it to colour before adding some of the wine. Scrape up all the brown bits from the bottom of the pan and pour into the casserole. Add the remaining wine, the marinade ingredients, salt and pepper, allspice and enough stock to cover the hare. Bring to a simmer on top of the stove before covering and placing in a oven preheated to 170°C/325°F/gas 3 for about 1 hour.

Meanwhile add the butter to the frying pan and gently sauté the onions, covered, for 10 minutes. Uncover and glaze the onions. Remove the onions from the pan and add the mushrooms. Season and stir until they are lightly coloured. Add both mushrooms and onions to the hare for the last 20 minutes of the cooking time.

Mix the blood with the cream and incorporate it into the stew, being careful to keep the sauce below boiling point. The stew can be heated slightly so it thickens, but do not allow it to boil or it will separate.

Serve with the fried bread and a sprinkling of parsley.

Hare Sauce for Pasta

Henrietta Green's excellent hare sauce for pasta.

serves 5–6

2 rashers of smoked bacon, de-rinded and chopped	1 teaspoon chopped fresh thyme
3 tablespoons of olive oil	1 teaspoon fresh winter savory
30 g (1 oz) unsalted butter	1 teaspoon chopped fresh parsley
1 garlic clove, crushed	150 ml ($\frac{1}{4}$ pint) meat or game stock
1 onion, chopped	150 ml ($\frac{1}{4}$ pint) red wine
1 celery stalk, chopped	150 ml ($\frac{1}{4}$ pint) double cream
1 carrot, sliced	salt and freshly ground black pepper
hindquarters of 1 hare	450 g (1 lb) tagliatelle
2 teaspoons flour	85 g (3 oz) freshly grated parmesan cheese
1 teaspoon chopped fresh rosemary	

Sauté the bacon in the oil and butter for 1 minute. Add the garlic, onion, celery, and carrot and cook a further 2 minutes. Add the hare legs and sauté on all sides until lightly browned, sprinkle over the flour and cook for a further minute, stirring continually. Add the herbs, pour over the stock and wine and bring to the boil. Reduce the heat to a gentle simmer, cover, and cook for 1½ hours or until the hare is tender. Top up with more stock if necessary. Remove the legs from the pan, strip the meat off the bone, and cut into dice. Return the diced meat to the pan, stir in the cream, heat it gently and season to taste. Serve with a bowl of tagliatelle and parmesan cheese.

Saddle of Hare with Italia Grapes

Italia grapes with their lovely muscatel flavour combine most deliciously with game of all sorts – partridge, pheasant, grouse and guail. This recipe is adapted from a recipe by Eckart Witzigmann in *La Nouvelle Cuisine Allemande et Autrichienne* (1984). Recipes such as this can easily be tackled for dinner parties. If grapes are pipped and shallots chopped in advance, the sauce is much the same and just as quick as making a gravy from a roast.

serves 4

1 saddle of hare
25 g (¾ oz) butter
salt and pepper

For the marinade:
1 carrot, chopped
1 stalk of celery, chopped
2 tablespoons olive oil
a few parsley stalks, chopped
2 sprigs of thyme
bay leaf
1 clove
3 tablespoons sauternes

For the sauce:
1 shallot, finely chopped
1 tablespoon wine vinegar
200 ml (good ¼ pint) crème fraîche
juice of half a lemon
200 g (7 oz) Italia grapes, skinned, halved and pipped
30 g (1 oz) unsalted butter
salt and pepper

Marinate the saddle for 2 days in the marinade ingredients. Strain and reserve marinade. Remove the thin skin over the saddle with a sharp knife. Ease the fillets away from the chine bone, without removing them, to make carving easier. Heat the 25 g (¾ oz) of butter in a heavy roasting pan until it foams. Place the saddle on the butter and set in an oven preheated to 220°C/425°F/gas 7. Roast for 15 minutes. Remove the saddle to a heated dish, season and leave to rest while you make the sauce.

125

Deglaze the roasting pan, stir in the shallot and when it begins to colour add the vinegar and reduce until dry. Strain the marinade into the pan and again reduce until almost dry. Add the cream and simmer until it thickens slightly. Strain the sauce (through a chinois if possible) into a small saucepan. Season with salt, pepper and a squeeze of lemon juice. Swirl in the butter and add the grapes. Carve the saddle and serve the slices with some sauce spooned over them.

Italian Civet of Hare

serves 6–8

1 hare, jointed or 2.75 kg (6 lb) of hare pieces plus blood, if possible
3 tablespoons olive oil
85 g (3 oz) butter
3 onions, roughly chopped
2 sticks of celery, sliced
2 carrots sliced
branch of fresh rosemary or 2 teaspoons of dried rosemary
bouquet garni
1 bottle Barolo or other strong red wine
$\frac{1}{2}$ teaspoon cayenne
salt and freshly ground black pepper

Wipe the hare dry, season and brown in the oil and butter. Transfer to a large flame-proof casserole. Pour off the fat from the pan, deglaze with a little of the wine and pour over hare. Add vegetables, rosemary, cayenne, salt and pepper and the rest of the wine to the casserole. Bring to the boil, cover, and simmer gently for about 2 hours, or until tender. Turn the pieces of hare once or twice during the simmering time. Remove hare to a heated dish. Strain the sauce into a saucepan, pressing on the vegetables to extract all the juices. Adjust seasoning and stir in the blood, if you are using it. Stir over low heat until sauce thickens (do not boil), ladle some sauce over the hare and serve the rest separately.

VENISON
AND WILD BOAR

Venison and Wild Boar

THE THREE TYPES of venison most readily available in Great Britain are the Red deer, Fallow deer and Roe deer. The Red deer is the largest of the three and tends to have the strongest, richest flavour. The Roe deer (*chevreuil* in French), is a small delicate animal that is the most tender of the three. The Fallow comes somewhere in between in both flavour and size.

Ancient Egyptians, Israelites, Greeks and Romans all kept deer, and we can thank the Romans for introducing the fallow deer, like so much else, to this country. In Medieval Britain there were numerous deer parks – almost 2000 at one time in England alone – which were partly maintained for sport but primarily to stock the table. The Civil War in the mid-seventeenth century put an end to many parks, while the few that remained became merely decorative. There was always a certain amount of hunting, both of wild and carted deer (those taken by cart to a starting point for the hunt), and deer also graced the parks of grand houses. But there was little or no farming of deer.

Scotland has traditionally been the favoured location for deer stalking, though it has always been a sport for the few. It was however encouraged by the romantic enthusiasm largely engendered, in the nineteenth century, by Queen Victoria's love of Scotland and Highland life. The romantic novels of Walter Scott, the paintings of Landseer and the poems of Robert Burns ('My heart's in the Highlands, my heart is not here. My heart's in the Highlands, a-chasing the deer') all contributed to this enthusiasm. Stalking, however, did not provide enough venison for the general food markets.

In this century, as land development increased and the woodlands were reduced, deer became scare in Britain except for the comparatively small herds in parks. In the 1960s, when farmers sought alternative uses for their land, deer farming began again after a lapse of centuries.

The appetite for venison has increased steadily, not only because of its fine flavour but also because of its low fat content. Most farmed venison is 18 months old when it is sold. At that age the animal fat will be as low as 5%, compared to the fat content of beef, which is 20%, or lamb, which is 25%. In addition, half of venison fat consists of polyunsaturates. A slight drawback is its high melting point. Like lamb, venison must be served on very hot plates and pan juices assiduously skimmed.

There is much talk of the relative value of farmed and wild venison. Farmed venison should be tender, but stalked or hunted venison will be more variable and less predictable. When in doubt as to the origins, marinate the meat before cooking. This will help tenderise the meat and mellow the flavour. Because the meat is so lean, even joints cut from young animals will need to be larded and basted. The best joints are the saddle and haunch, which are usually roasted or cut into chops and grilled. These joints should be served underdone so they will be juicy. A well-done roast of venison can be dry because of the lack of fat and therefore disappointing. The neck, breast and shoulder are ideal for casseroles.

The liver, particularly from the roe deer, has long been considered a great delicacy in Europe and is now appearing on restaurant menus in Britain.

THE WILD BOAR became extinct in England in the seventeenth century but it is still to be found in deciduous forests and scrub land in many parts of Europe and Asia where its flavour is much appreciated. Today, in Britain, enterprising farmers have successfully cross-bred wild boar with the Tamworth pig. (Pure-bred boars need a dangerous-animal certificate which makes a whole herd of them impractical.) The cross-bred boar are fed on a natural diet of acorns, apples, beechmast and barley and their slow growth makes for excellent flavour.

Recipes for pork can be used for boar but bear in mind that its stronger flavour can be enhanced by sharp fruit or a well seasoned sauce.

— •●• —

11 ## Roast Haunch of Venison

Roasting a leg of venison is no more complicated than roasting any other joint and the meat has a lovely delicate flavour, not at all over-powering. The only precaution it is wise to take is to cover it in caul, or pork back fat or lard it. The latter is not tricky but just means you have to have a larding needle and strips of pork back fat. It is very satisfying to see the bits of pork neatly stitched over the surface and feel confident that the joint will be succulent. Harrods and other good butchers will lard venison on request. Serve the venison with a parsley purée and a potato and celeriac gratin – both can be made in advance.

serves 12

3.6–4.1 kg (8–9 lb) haunch of roe or fallow venison

For the larding
pork back fat, cut into 5 mm ($\frac{1}{4}$ inch) strips or caul or pork back fat to cover haunch

For the marinade
4 tablespoons olive oil
5 tablespoons dry white wine
2 tablespoons dried provençal herbs (thyme, oregano and savory)

For the sauce
1 shallot, very finely chopped
1 tablespoon oil
1 carrot, finely chopped
5 mushrooms, very finely chopped
5 tablespoons cognac
110 ml (scant $\frac{1}{4}$ pint) madeira
600 ml (1 pint) good game stock
1 tablespoon arrowroot
salt and pepper

To lard the haunch: Thread the needle with a strip of the fat. Lard the round side of the meat by taking single, shallow stitches about 3.8 cm ($3\frac{1}{2}$ inches) long. Cut the ends of the lard slightly larger than the stitch. Cover the surface with stitches about 2.5 cm (1 inch) apart.

Place the meat on a large piece of foil. Pour over the marinade: rub in the herbs. Cover with foil and leave for at least 6 hours or overnight.

For the sauce sauté the shallot and carrot in the oil, stirring, for a couple of minutes. Add the mushrooms, and sauté a few more minutes. Pour in the cognac and reduce by half. Add the madeira and stock, and simmer gently for 5 minutes. Strain into a clean saucepan and season to taste. The recipe can be made in advance up to this point. Refrigerate the sauce, covered if not to be used the same day.

Leave the meat at room temperature. Preheat the oven to 220°C/425°F/gas 7. Place meat in a roasting tin and pour over the marinade. Roast for 20 minutes, then reduce the oven to 180°C/350°F/gas 4. Allow 10 minutes per 450 g (1 lb), including the initial searing time. Baste a few times with olive oil. Remove from the oven and rest for 15 minutes before serving.

Reheat the sauce. Pour away any fat from the roasting tin and deglaze with some of the sauce, then strain into the rest of the sauce. Mix the arrowroot with 2 tablespoons of water, add to the sauce and simmer a few minutes. Check the seasoning and serve.

Spicy Venison Stew

serves 6

4 tablespoons olive oil	$\frac{1}{2}$ teaspoon oregano
925 g (2 lb) cubed venison, from shoulder or neck	bay leaf
1 large onion chopped	300 ml ($\frac{1}{2}$ pint) red wine
1 chilli pepper, seeded and chopped	600 ml (1 pint) beef stock
5 cloves garlic	1 kg (35 oz) can of chopped tomatoes
2 teaspoons cumin seeds	170 g (6 oz) frozen corn, off the cob
1 tablespoon paprika	5 spring onions, chopped
$\frac{1}{2}$ teaspoon cayenne	salt and pepper

Pat the meat dry, and season with salt and pepper. Heat 3 tablespoons of the oil in a heavy frying pan and brown the meat on all sides. Transfer the meat with a slotted spoon to a flameproof casserole. Add the remaining oil, onion, chilli, and garlic to the pan and cook gently to soften the vegetables. Add the cumin, paprika and cayenne and cook for 30 seconds. Add the red wine, deglaze the pan and add to the casserole. Add the tomatoes, stock, oregano and bay leaf to the casserole. Bring to a simmer on top of the stove before covering and barely simmering in a 150°C/300°F/gas 2 oven for 2 hours or until the meat is tender. Add the sweetcorn and cook for another 10 minutes. Adjust the seasoning, stir in the spring onions, and serve.

Venison Chilli

Recipes for venison chilli are frequent in American cookbooks and indeed venison is ideally suited for the spicy flavours of a chilli. The amount of chillies to use depends on what sort of heat you are after. It is nice to serve side dishes of yoghurt, grated cheddar cheese, chopped lettuce, chopped tomatoes and chopped coriander.

serves 12

For the beans
450 g (1 lb) dried red kidney or
    pinto beans
2 cloves garlic, crushed
2 teaspoons salt
2 tablespoons groundnut oil
1 large onion, finely chopped
2 fresh green chillies

For the meat
2 kg ($4\frac{1}{2}$ lbs) cubed venison, from
    shoulder or neck

6 tablespoons olive oil
3 tablespoons flour
$\frac{1}{2}$-1 tablespoon cayenne pepper
2 teaspoons cumin seeds
2 teaspoons oregano
1-3 chillies, seeded and finely
    chopped
6 cloves garlic, finely chopped
1 litre ($1\frac{3}{4}$ pints) beef stock
fresh coriander leaves, chopped
salt and freshly ground black
    pepper

Soak the beans in water overnight, covering them with several inches of water. Rinse the beans, then place in a heavy saucepan with 2.4 litres (4 pints) of water and the garlic. Boil for about 3 hours or until beans are tender. Top up with water if necessary. Add the salt and cook a further 10 minutes. Meanwhile fry the onion in the oil until golden, add the chillies and simmer another 10 minutes. Discard the chillies. If beans are too watery spoon off some water and add the onions and oil. Cool and refrigerate (up to one week) until needed.

Heat the oil in a deep flameproof casserole. Add the meat and stir over medium-high heat until the meat loses its red colour. Stir the cayenne and teaspoon of salt into the flour. Sieve over the meat and stir to distribute evenly. Shake the cumin seeds in a small heavy hot frying pan for a few minutes so they colour. Add the cumin, oregano, garlic, chillies, freshly ground black pepper and stock to the meat. Simmer very gently for 3-4 hours, or until meat almost falls apart. Add more stock if necessary and simmer uncovered if there is to much liquid at the end of the cooking time. Stir in the beans and heat if necessary. Taste for seasoning, decorate with coriander and serve.

Venison with Black-eyed Beans, Mushrooms and Coriander

The black-eyed beans with mushrooms element in this dish is inspired by a recipe of Madhur Jaffrey's in *Indian Cookery*. Follow it with a green salad and fresh fruit such as mango.

serves 8

For the meat
900 g (2 lb) cubed venison from
   shoulder or neck
seasoned flour
4 tablespoons olive oil
1 onion, chopped
1 carrot, chopped
1 stick of celery, chopped
5 juniper berries, crushed
bouquet garni
glass of red wine
300 ml ($\frac{1}{2}$ pint) game or beef stock.

For the beans and mushrooms
225 g ($\frac{1}{2}$ lb) dried black-eyed beans
6 tablespoons ground nut oil

1 teaspoon cumin seeds
5 cm (2 inch) stick of cinnamon
1 large onion, finely chopped
4 cloves garlic, finely chopped
225 g ($\frac{1}{2}$ lb) mushrooms, sliced
2 teaspoons ground coriander seeds
1 teaspoons ground cumin
$\frac{1}{2}$ teaspoon cayenne pepper
$\frac{1}{2}$ teaspoon turmeric
400 g (14 oz) can of chopped
   tomatoes
2 teaspoons salt
freshly ground black pepper
4 tablespoons fresh coriander,
   chopped

For the venison; roll the meat in seasoned flour. Heat half the oil in a frying pan and brown. Transfer the meat to a heavy saucepan or flameproof casserole. Add the rest of the oil to the pan, stir in the vegetables and juniper berries and cook until they are soft. Deglaze with the wine then pour the contents of the pan over the meat. Add the bouquet garni and stock. Simmer very gently for $2\frac{1}{2}$ hours, or until tender. Top up with water or more stock if needed.

For the beans and mushrooms; pick over the beans, wash and drain and place in a saucepan with 1.15 litres (2 pints) of water. Bring to the boil, cover, and simmer for 2 minutes. Turn off the heat and leave, covered, for 1 hour. Meanwhile heat the oil in a heavy frying pan. Toss in the cumin seeds and cinnamon stick and fry for a few seconds, add the onions and garlic, stir and fry until the onions start to brown. Add the mushrooms, ground coriander, ground cumin, turmeric and cayenne. Stir and cook for a few minutes, add the tomatoes and simmer gently for 10 minutes. Remove from the heat and set aside.

Bring the beans to the boil again. Cover, reduce the heat and simmer very gently for 30 minutes, or until beans are tender. Add mushrooms, salt, ground pepper and half the coriander. Stir in the venison and reheat if necessary. Serve decorated with coriander.

Venison Meat Loaf

This is a versatile loaf that can be served hot or cold and also freezes well.

serves 8–10

450 g (1 lb) good quality sausages
450 g (1 lb) minced venison
60 g (2 oz) fresh white breadcrumbs
2 eggs
1 large red onion or mild spanish
  onion, finely chopped

150 ml ($\frac{1}{4}$ pint) whipping cream
70 g ($2\frac{1}{2}$ oz) shelled unsalted
  pistachio nuts
2 tablespoons chopped parsley
salt and freshly ground black pepper
150 ml ($\frac{1}{4}$ pint) milk

Cut open the sausage skins, scrape the meat into a large bowl and mix with the venison, breadcrumbs, eggs, cream, nuts and parsley. Make a small patty with the mixture and fry to test for seasoning. Season accordingly, then form into a loaf and place on a greased roasting tin. Bake in an oven preheated to 180°C/350°F/ gas 4 for 50 minutes. Baste at frequent intervals with the milk. This will curdle in the pan but take no notice. Remove the loaf to a heated platter. Pour off the fat from the pan but leave the curds. Deglaze the pan with a few tablespoons of water scraping up all the curds and bits from the pan. Slice the loaf and pour the pan juices over the slices. Red cabbage, chestnut purée, and the usual vegetables that go well with venison can accompany the venison loaf. Cranberry sauce can be served with cold slices of the meat loaf.

Peppered Saddle of Venison

serves 8

3 kg (6 lb 9 oz) saddle of
   roe venison
30 g (1 oz) black peppercorns
12 juniper berries
6 tablespoons olive oil
6 tablespoons butter
3 tablespoons brandy

150 ml ($\frac{1}{4}$ pint) red wine
250 ml (scant $\frac{1}{2}$ pint) game or
   veal stock
150 ml ($\frac{1}{4}$ pint) double cream
2 teaspoons arrowroot (optional)
salt

Carefully remove the skin from the venison saddle, only just leaving the flesh exposed. Crush the peppercorns and juniper berries in a mortar. Brush the saddle with olive oil and press a thin coating of the peppercorn mixture into the flesh. Leave in a cool place for 8 hours or overnight.

Preheat the oven to 220°C/425°F/gas 7. Pour a little oil in a roasting tin and heat until the oil is very hot. Dot the top of the pepper-encrusted venison with butter and set in the tin. Roast for 35–40 minutes, basting at intervals. Place on a warm serving dish, and cover loosely with foil.

Pour away any fat from the tin, deglaze with the brandy, then add the wine and reduce by half. Add the stock and boil hard for a minute or two. Add the cream and season with salt. The sauce can be thickened with 2 teaspoons of arrowroot slaked in a bit of water, then added to the sauce and simmered for a minute. If the saddle has not been chined, remove the 2 large top fillets and carve into noisettes. The smaller bottom fillets can be sliced into long thin pieces. Serve with some sauce spooned around the meat.

———— •●• ————

CIPD Enterprises L...
CIPD House Camp Road Londc
Tel: 020 8971 9000 Fax: 020 826
Registered office as stated Registere

Venison Liver with Wine Sauce

... is from Chef-patron David Wilson of the Peat Inn, Fife.
...ence he would use roe deer liver which has a mild delicate
... – much appreciated in central Europe. The liver of the red
...as a stronger flavour but can be used in the same way.

serves 4

450 g (16 oz) venison liver,
   thinly sliced
ground nut oil for frying
4 tablespoons finely chopped onion
1 tablespoon sherry vinegar
1 tablespoon caster sugar
150 ml ($\frac{1}{4}$ pint) red wine

300 ml ($\frac{1}{2}$ pint) strong meat stock
60 g (2 oz) cold unsalted butter,
   cubed
2 tablespoons peeled and diced
   potato
salt and pepper

Sauté 2 tablespoons of the onion in a very little oil until soft, add the sugar, red wine and vinegar. Reduce until almost evaporated, then add the stock. Simmer gently to concentrate the flavour and reduce slightly. Set aside. The sauce can be prepared up to this point several hours ahead.

Cook the potato and second 2 tablespoons of onion in oil until they are crisp and golden. Drain on kitchen paper and keep warm, (this too can be done in advance and reheated before serving).

At the last moment before serving season the liver with salt and pepper. Heat the oil in a sauté pan and cook the slices briefly on each side. They should be nicely browned on the outside but kept rosy inside. Drain on kitchen paper and keep warm for a few minutes while you finish the sauce. Reheat the sauce then whisk in the cubed butter, on and off the heat, to thicken the sauce. Season to taste.

Spoon some sauce on heated plates. Place the liver slices on the sauce. Season the fried potato and onion mixture and strew over the liver. Serve immediately.

——— ••• ———

Venison Stew

A wonderful dish for the winter and special enough to be party fare. It improves with reheating, so can be made well in advance. It makes excellent filling for pies, and individual pies made with light home-made puff pastry would be worth considering for a special occasion.

serves 8

$1\frac{1}{2}$ kilos (3 lb) cubed venison, from shoulder or neck
300 ml ($\frac{1}{2}$ pint) red wine
3 tablespoons olive oil
bouquet garni
$\frac{1}{4}$ teaspoon crushed black peppercorns
250 g (8 oz) pancetta, or piece of streaky bacon, cut into lardons
2 shallots, finely chopped
1 large onion, finely chopped
2 stalks of celery, finely chopped
2 carrots, finely chopped
1 clove garlic, crushed then chopped

45 g ($1\frac{1}{2}$ oz) unsalted butter
2 tablespoons flour
2 tablespoons brandy
500 ml (1 pint) beef or venison stock
bouquet garni
45 g ($1\frac{1}{2}$ oz) butter
34 pickling onions
1 tablespoon raspberry vinegar
1 teaspoon sugar
450 g (1 lb) button mushrooms
1 tablespoon olive oil
lemon juice
salt and pepper
finely chopped parsley to decorate

Mix the red wine, olive oil, bouquet garni and peppercorns with the venison and marinate for 24 hours in a cool place. Drain off and keep the marinade. Brown the bacon in a heavy frying pan, remove with a slotted spoon to a flameproof casserole. Tip out all but about 2 table-spoons of the bacon fat and brown the chopped vegetables; transfer to the casserole. Turn the venison in the flour. Heat half the butter in the pan and brown the venison cubes in batches, transferring them to the casserole as you go. Pour away the fat from the pan and add the brandy. When this has evaporated pour in the strained marinade, scraping up any bits from the bottom of the pan. Pour this over the venison, adding the stock and bouquet garni. Bring to a simmer on top of the stove before covering with a sheet of greaseproof paper and then the lid. Simmer very gently in a low oven 150°C/300°F/gas 2 for about 2 hours.

Meanwhile place the onions in a sauté pan just large enough to hold them in one layer. Add the remaining butter, sugar, vinegar and 6 tablespoons of water. Cook very slowly, covered, shaking the pan occasionally, until the onions are cooked and the liquid evaporated. Sauté the mushrooms in the olive oil, seasoning them with salt and pepper and lemon juice. Add onions and mushrooms to the venison before serving, and decorate with parsley.

Noisettes of Venison with Pear and Sorrel

serves 4

2 passacrassana or William pears
juice of $\frac{1}{2}$ lemon
2 tablespoons sugar
8 noisettes of venison, cut from
    loin or saddle
2 shallots, finely chopped
4 tablespoons oil

3 tablespoons madeira
300 ml ($\frac{1}{2}$ pint) beef or venison stock
3 tablespoons fresh sorrel leaves,
    without centre stalks, finely
    chopped
30 g (1 oz) cold unsalted butter,
    diced
salt and pepper

Peel, halve, and poach the pears in 300 ml ($\frac{1}{2}$ pint) of water, the lemon juice and sugar. Save half of the peel.

Sauté the shallots in one tablespoon of the oil until golden. Deglaze with the Madeira, add the stock and half the pear peelings and simmer for 8 minutes. Strain into a clean saucepan and add half of the sorrel. Season the venison. Heat the remaining oil in a heavy frying pan and when it is very hot sear the meat for about 1 minute each side. Reduce the heat to medium and sauté for a further 4–5 minutes each side. Place on heated plates and keep warm. Pour away all the fat and blot up excess with kitchen paper. Deglaze with a little sauce, pour back into the sauce, bring to a simmer and add the rest of the sorrel. Whisk in the butter, on and off the heat so the butter thickens the sauce. Adjust the seasoning. Quickly reheat the pears and cut into slices. Spoon some sauce over the noisettes and decorate with a few slices of pear.

Venison Crepinettes

serves 6

For the sauce
6 cloves garlic, very finely chopped
1 tablespoon unsalted butter
300 ml ($\frac{1}{2}$ pint) single cream
1 tablespoon finely chopped
  parsley
salt and freshly ground black
  pepper
6 thick venison medallions, from
  boned-out loin fillet of fallow or
  roe deer

1 shallot, finely chopped
350 g (12 oz) mushrooms,
  finely chopped
oil
squeeze of lemon juice
1 teaspoon finely chopped parsley
2 large pieces of caul fat
salt and freshly ground black
  pepper

To make the sauce; place the garlic and butter in a small thick-bottomed saucepan and simmer gently over low heat until the garlic begins to soften. Do not allow it to colour. Add the cream and continue to simmer gently for about 10 minutes, until the cream thickens slightly and is flavoured with the garlic. Season with salt and pepper and strain into a clean saucepan. Before serving the sauce reheat gently and stir in the parsley.

Using a frying pan, sweat the shallot in one tablespoon of oil, stir in the mushrooms and season with lemon juice, salt and pepper. Continue to cook until the liquid from the mushrooms has evaporated and you are left with quite a dry mixture. Cool, then add the parsley.

Season and seal the venison seaks very briefly in hot oil. Rinse the caul fat in warm water to make it supple. Stretch it out on a flat surface and cut 6 squares, each large enough to enclose a medallion. Place a bed of the mushrooms in the centre of the squares, set the meat on top and spoon over the rest of the mushrooms. Wrap the caul around to make a parcel. Place in a hot, greased pan in a hot oven preheated to 230°C/450°F/gas 8 for 10–12 minutes. Serve with a purée of celeriac or swede.

Note: the garlic sauce makes a easy and very good pasta sauce. Try it with fresh tagliatelle.

Cotelettes de Chevreuil à l'Ardennaise

This dish is inspired by a recipe from Elizabeth David's *French Provincial Cooking*.

serves 6

6 thick boned venison chops,
    cut from the saddle of a roe deer
12, juniper berries, crushed
8 black peppercorns, crushed
$\frac{1}{2}$ teaspoon dried thyme
salt
squeeze of lemon juice
3 shallots, chopped
1 carrot, diced

1 stick of celery, diced
unsalted butter
200 ml (scant $\frac{1}{2}$ pint) dry white
    wine
125 ml (scant $\frac{1}{4}$ pint) game stock
6 dessertspoons chopped cooked
    ham
6 dessertspoons breadcrumbs
3 tablespoons chopped parsley

Place the meat in a shallow dish, squeeze the lemon juice over the chops, turning them so both sides are impregnated. Mix the juniper berries, peppercorns and thyme with some salt and rub into the chops. Leave for 2 hours.

Place a knob of butter in a frying pan, add the vegetables and sweat them until they are lightly coloured. Remove the vegetables to a shallow oven dish large enough to hold the meat in one layer. Brown the chops in the pan, and place them over the vegetables. Deglaze the frying pan with the wine, reduce by half and pour over the chops. Cover the meat with a layer of ham then top with a mixture of breadcrumbs and parsley. Dot the top of each chop with butter, pour the stock around the edge and bake, uncovered, in an oven preheated to 150°C/300°F/gas 2 for $1\frac{3}{4}$ hours, or until the meat is tender. Serve with a purée of chestnuts or celeriac and potatoes (Chapter 12).

Marinated Shoulder of Venison

The shoulder will have very good flavour but will shrink considerably during the long braising time.

serves 4–6

Marinade;
150 ml ($\frac{1}{4}$ pint) each red wine
  vinegar and red wine
1 large onion, sliced
2 bay leaves
stalk of celery, chopped
level teaspoon each of juniper
  berries and black pepper,
  crushed
2 kg (4 lb) boned shoulder of
  venison

oil
slices of fat bacon
1 small onion, carrot, celery and
  leek, all diced
300 ml ($\frac{1}{2}$ pint) game stock
150 ml ($\frac{1}{4}$ pint) soured cream
60 g (2 oz) gingernut biscuits,
  crumbled

Bring marinade to the boil, cool, then pour over the venison. Cover and leave in a cool larder or the bottom of the refrigerator for 3–5 days, turning once or twice daily.

Brown the meat in a few tablespoons of oil in a sauté pan, then remove the meat to an oval earthenware dish in which it will fit snugly. Cover the meat in strips of bacon. Brown the diced vegetables in the sauté pan and place on top of the meat. Pour over the strained marinade and season with salt. Cover with a round of greaseproof paper and then the lid. Cook in a very slow oven, 150°C/ 300°F/ gas 2, for about 2$\frac{1}{2}$ hours. Remove the meat to a heated plate and cover loosely with foil. Strain the liquid into a pan, pressing on the vegetables to extract all the flavour. Boil to reduce it slightly, then thicken with the cream and crushed gingernuts, and adjust the seasoning. Carve the meat into thin slices and serve with the sauce. Red cabbage and a potato purée (Chapter 12) would go well with this dish.

Venison with Balsamic Vinegar Sauce

The availability of subtle-flavoured vinegars have enlarged the possibility of easy tasty sauces which require no stocks or reductions.

serves 2

1 tablespoon balsamic vinegar	2 venison steaks or chops
2 tablespoons extra virgin olive oil	25 g (1 oz) unsalted butter, cut into small pieces
1 teaspoon fresh rosemary, chopped	salt and coarsely ground black pepper
1 small pinch of oregano	
pinch of cayenne	

Place the vinegar, oil, rosemary, oregano and cayenne in a small saucepan and whisk over gentle heat until hot. Remove from the heat and set aside while you grill your meat – either in a pan or under a grill. Reheat the sauce and whisk in the butter, bit by bit, off and on the heat so the butter thickens rather than melts the sauce. Pour over your steak and serve.

Venison Chops with Dried Fruit and Mushrooms

When vinegar is called for in making a sauce it is crucial that a mild one is used or it will dominate the other ingredients. Start with less than the given amount if you are in doubt about the strength of your vinegar. *Never* use malt or pickling vinegar.

serves 4

8 prunes	85 g (3 oz) butter
12 dried apricots	8 venison chops
1 China tea bag	2–3 tablespoons mild wine vinegar
450 g (1 lb) shiitake mushrooms	60 g (2 oz) sugar
1 teaspoon coriander seeds	150 ml ($\frac{1}{4}$ pint) chicken stock
2 tablespoons oil	salt and freshly ground black pepper

Place the dried fruit and tea bag in a bowl, cover with boiling water and leave to soften. Slice the mushrooms. Heat one tablespoon each of oil and butter in a frying pan and sauté the mushrooms and coriander. Add a pinch of salt, a few grindings of pepper and cook over a very gentle heat for about 10 minutes. Dry the chops with kitchen paper and season lightly. Heat another tablespoon each of oil and butter and when it is very hot sauté the chops for about 6 minutes each side. Keep them on the pink side. Remove the chops to a heated serving dish and keep warm. Pour away any fat from the pan and add the sugar. Cook the sugar until it caramelises and is a good rich brown colour. Pour in the vinegar (keep your face averted, because it spits), and stir with a wooden spoon until the mixture blends. Add the stock and reduce a little. Swirl bits of the butter into the sauce, off and on the heat so the butter thickens the sauce without melting. Adjust the seasoning. Quickly reheat the mushrooms and the fruit and arrange on either side of the venison. Spoon some sauce over the meat and serve.

Venison Steaks With Redcurrants

Both pigeon and duck breasts are very good dealt with in this easy manner.

serves 4

4 venison steaks about 140 g (5 oz) each
2 tablespoon oil
40 g ($1\frac{1}{2}$ oz) unsalted butter
1 shallot, chopped very fine
$\frac{1}{2}$ carrot, chopped very fine
$\frac{1}{2}$ stick celery, chopped very fine

1 tablespoon red wine vinegar
1 tablespoon redcurrant jelly
150 ml ($\frac{1}{4}$ pint) game stock
50 g (2 oz) fresh redcurrants, stemmed
salt and pepper

Heat 1 tablespoon of the butter in a small heavy saucepan, stir in the carrot and soften slightly before adding the shallot and celery. Continue to stir until the vegetables are soft and golden. Add the vinegar and evaporate it before stirring in the redcurrant jelly. Add the stock, simmer for a few minutes and remove from the heat.

Pour the oil into a heavy frying or gilling pan and heat until it is very hot. Season the steaks and sear them quickly on both sides, reduce the heat and sauté a few minutes more on each side. Keep them pink and tender. When the steaks are done remove them to a heated plate, pour away the fat from the pan and deglaze with the sauce. Cut the remaining butter into small pieces and swirl them into the sauce gradually so the sauce thickens. Add the fresh redcurrants to the sauce and serve immediately.

Wild Boar Sausages

Boar makes memorable sausages, and if you have a mincer and a sausage-making attachment for your food-processor nothing could be easier. There is endless scope for different seasonings such as juniper berries, garlic, sage, shallots and fresh herbs.

to make 680 g (1½ lbs)

450 g (1 lb) lean boar meat, from the shoulder or loin
225 g (½ lb) fresh boar or pork back fat
1½ teaspoons fine sea salt

freshly ground black pepper
small pinch of ground cloves and nutmeg
2 tablespoons fennel seed
sausage casings

Soak the casings overnight in cold water. Mince the meat and fat then mix in the seasonings and 4 tablespoons of cold water. Run cold water through the casing then push on to the nozzle of a sausage-making machine. Don't fill the casing too tightly, and let it fall in a coil or twist into links. Place the sausages in a frying pan and add water to come half way up the sausages. Boil until the water evaporates, turning the sausages once or twice. Alternatively the sausages can be grilled or fried.

Note: Venison sausages are made in the same way using lean venison meat and fresh pork back fat in the same proportions as above. Black-eyed beans go well with both kinds of sausages and the recipe for Venison with Black-eyed beans, Mushrooms and Coriander earlier in this chapter can be used, omitting the venison in the recipe.

Leg of Pork à la Sanglier

A long marinade in wine and aromatic vegetables can transform the taste of pork to a more gamey one. Plan ahead, as it will need to be left 4 days in the marinade.

serves 10

2.75 kg (6 lb) boned leg of pork

For the marinade
450 ml ($\frac{3}{4}$ pint) red wine
6 tablespoons cider vinegar
2 carrots, chopped
1 onion, chopped
1 stalk of celery, chopped
4 cloves garlic, crushed
9 juniper berries, crushed
10 black peppercorns, crushed
large bouquet garni with lots of
    parsley stalks, 2 sprigs of thyme
    and 2 bay leaves
1 tablespoon salt

For cooking
3 shallots, chopped
1 carrot, chopped
1 stalk celery, chopped
chopped parsley
olive oil
300 ml ($\frac{1}{2}$ pint) veal stock
arrowroot
salt and freshly ground black
    pepper

Skin the meat, score the fat and place the meat in a china or glass bowl. Boil all the marinade ingredients together for 5 minutes, cool, then pour over the pork and cover with cling-film or a lid. Store in a cool place. Leave for 4 days, turning the pork twice a day in the liquid.

Take the meat out of the marinade, remove any of the vegetables that may be clinging to it and wipe dry. Brown the cooking vegetables and parsley in some oil and place in the bottom of a large flameproof casserole. Brown the pork on all sides and set on top of the vegetables. Strain the marinade over the meat and add the stock. Bring to a simmer on top of the stove, cover with a sheet of greaseproof paper and a lid. Simmer gently in a low oven 160°C/325°F/gas 3 for 2–2$\frac{1}{2}$ hours. Turn the meat over half-way through the cooking time. Place the meat on a hot serving dish. Spoon off all the surface fat from the cooking liquid and boil hard to concentrate the flavour, then adjust the seasoning. The sauce can be thickened with a little slaked arrowroot if desired. Serve with redcurrant jelly and any of the vegetables that go well with game such as lentils, chestnuts or celeriac (Chapter 12).

Note: A leg of lamb can be treated in the same manner to transform it into 'venison'.

Sweet and Sour Wild Boar

Chocolate is frequently used in Italian game dishes. It adds a mysterious rich flavour that is not easily recognisable. This recipe is one of Jane Grigson's.

serves 8

1.35 kg (3 lb) boned leg of wild
    boar
seasoned flour

For the marinade
375 ml ($\frac{3}{4}$ pint) red wine
medium carrot and onion,
    chopped
bouquet garni
3 cloves
salt and freshly ground black
    pepper

For the sauce
60 g (2 oz) diced fat streaky bacon
game, veal, or beef stock
$1\frac{1}{2}$ tablespoons sugar
3 tablespoons wine vinegar
up to 60 g (2 oz) sultanas
up to 60 g (2 oz) candied citrus
    peel, cut in strips
30 g (1 oz) pine kernels
15–30 g ($\frac{1}{2}$–1 oz) top quality bitter
    or plain chocolate
salt and freshly ground black pepper
lemon juice

Marinate the meat in the marinade ingredients for at least 4 hours and up to 2 days. Pat meat dry and roll in the seasoned flour. Fry the bacon in a heavy pan. Brown the meat in the bacon fat, pushing the bacon to one side. Transfer boar and bacon to a deep flameproof casserole with a close-fitting lid. Add the marinade with its bits and enough stock to bring the liquid level about three-quarters of the way up the side of the meat. Bring to a boil, cover, lower the heat so it cooks at a gentle simmer; turn the meat twice, allowing $1\frac{1}{2}$ hours or until it is tender, but do not overcook especially if the dish is to be reheated.

Transfer the meat to a dish and leave to relax in a low oven while you finish the sauce.

Skim the fat from the cooking liquor, strain into a pan, and boil down to concentrate the flavour.

Meanwhile dissolve sugar in a little water in a small heavy saucepan and cook to the caramel stage. Remove pan from the heat, stir in

147

the vinegar (keeping the face averted, as it spits), and place back on the heat to dissolve the sugar. Add to the reduced liquor, taste and stir in half the sultanas, peel, pine kernels and chocolate. Simmer 5 minutes. Taste and add as much of the rest of these items as pleases you. Season with salt, pepper and lemon juice.

If serving the next day: slice the boar and arrange in an ovenproof serving dish. Pour over the sauce, cover and chill when cool. Reheat, uncovered, in a moderate oven. If there is a good amount of sauce remove some to a separate bowl for serving.

To serve immediately: slice the boar on to a hot serving dish. Spoon over some of the sauce, and serve the rest separately. Grilled polenta (chapter 12) goes well with this dish.

PÂTÉS, PUDDINGS AND PIES

Pâtés, Puddings and Pies

Potted Hare

serves 6–8

230 g (8 oz) cooked boned hare
175 g (6 oz) unsalted butter at
   room temperature

1 tablespoon marsala
1 tablespoon rum
salt, pepper and cayenne

Chop the meat roughly and process with the butter until smooth. Mix alcohols into the pâté, and season to taste. Pack into a terrine, cover with cling-film and chill for at least 2 hours. Seal with a layer of melted butter if keeping for more than a day or so. Serve with toast.

Rabbit and Olive Pie

serves 4

680 g (1½ lb) boned rabbit meat
   including the liver and kidneys
2 tablespoons oil
1 tablespoons butter
1 tablespoon flour
300 ml (1½ pint) well reduced
   chicken or rabbit stock made
   from the bones
1 teaspoon fresh sage, finely
   chopped

4 crushed juniper berries
2 tablespoons cognac
12 black olives, stoned and
   quartered
4 tomatoes, skinned, seeded and
   chopped
340 g (¾ lb) puff pastry
1 egg mixed with a little water for
   glazing
salt and pepper

Chop the meat and innards into small pieces. Heat the butter and oil in a frying pan and lightly brown the meat. Season and sift over the flour. Stir in the stock, gradually cooking until it thickens. Turn into a bowl and mix with the sage, juniper berries, cognac, olives, tomatoes, salt and pepper. Leave to cool. Divide the pastry in half and roll out into 2 circles to fit a 25.5 cm (10 inch) diameter pie tin. Line the tin and fill with the rabbit mixture. Cover with pastry, pressing edges together to seal. Decorate with any remaining pastry.

Cut a few slits on the top to allow the steam to escape, glaze with the egg wash and bake in a preheated oven 220°C/425°F/gas 7 for 10 minutes. Lower the temperature to 180°C/350°F/gas 4 and bake for another 50 minutes. Cover the top of the pastry with foil if it becomes too dark. Serve with a green salad.

Compôte of Rabbit with Prunes

This quite delectable compôte is one of Lucien Vanel's, from his restaurant in Toulouse. Paula Wolfert has adapted it in '*The Cooking of South-West France*' 1988. It is like a super-light *rillette* and quite superb spread on toast.

serves 8 as a first course

1.50 kg (3¼ lb) rabbit joints

For the marinade
500 ml (scant pint) dry white wine
3 medium-sized onions, peeled and
    thinly slice
1 carrot, sliced
250 ml (scant ½ pint) olive oil,
1 shallot, sliced
1 clove garlic, halved

For the cooking
140 g (5 oz) salt pork cut into
    lardoons, (blanched if necessary)
oil
2 teaspoons dijon mustard
1.5 litres (2½ pints) chicken stock
bouquet garni
150 ml (¼ pint) double cream
15 young sorrel leaves shredded
lemon juice,
12 prunes
tea

Marinate rabbit overnight. Brown salt pork in a frying pan then transfer to a casserole. Brown the rabbit, adding oil as necessary, and spoon into the casserole, and then brown the marinade vegetables and add to the rabbit. Pour away the fat from the pan, stir in the mustard and deglaze with the strained marinade. Pour into the casserole along with the stock, bouquet garni, salt and freshly ground pepper. Cover and cook at 150°C/300°F/gas 2 for 4 hours, until the rabbit is falling off the bone. Strain liquid into a saucepan and degrease. Reduce a bit, then add the cream and reduce to 300 ml (½ pint). Remove the meat from the bones and shred. Place in a shallow dish. Add the sorrel to the sauce and bring to a boil. Pour over rabbit and cool. Season and refrigerate covered. The compôte will keep for a week. On the day of serving, soak the prunes in tea until swollen. Simmer a few minutes if necessary. Remove compôte from refrigerator 1 hour before serving and turn out. Serve surrounded by prunes.

Rabbit Rillettes with Hunza Apricots

Rillettes of one sort or another are a feature of charcuterie shops throughout France. They can be made from pork alone or a combination of pork and goose or rabbit. Confites such as these date back to at least the fifteenth century. The meat is cooked very slowly so it literally falls apart, it is then shredded to give it its attractive rough texture and sealed in fat. This can make a delicious first course served with crusty bread and the apricots.

serves 8–10

450 g (1 lb) lean pork, cubed	several gratings of nutmeg
1.35 kg (3 lbs) jointed rabbit, weighed with bone	2 bay leaves
	pinch of thyme
340 g ($\frac{3}{4}$ lb) fat pork (from the back), cubed	glass of dry white wine
	680 g ($1\frac{1}{2}$ lbs) dried hunza apricots
15 g ($\frac{1}{2}$ oz) salt	2 teaspoons finely chopped fresh
freshly ground black pepper	tarragon (optional)
pinch of ground allspice	

Place the pork, rabbit, fat pork, spices, wine and 300 ml ($\frac{1}{2}$ pint) of water in a heavy flame-proof casserole. Bring slowly to the boil, stirring steadily. Cover tightly and cook very slowly in an oven preheated to 160°C/320°F/gas $2\frac{1}{2}$, for 4–5 hours. Every hour or so, check on the moisture and add more water as necessary. The cooking can be done on top of the stove as well, as long as the heat is very low and even. Drain the meat, reserving the fat. Discard the bay leaves. Remove the rabbit meat from the bones and shred with the pork. The shredding should be done with 2 forks: do not process as the texture will be ruined. When the fat begins to cool add some of it to the meat, taste for seasoning then pack in a crock or glass jar. Heat the remaining fat and seal the *rillettes*. The *rillettes* can be kept for up to 2 weeks refrigerated.

Soak the apricots in water to cover overnight. Stone them, purée and sieve. Stir in the tarragon. Serve the apricot compôte with the rillettes.

Note: A prune purée, or any of the fruit compôtes would be equally delicious with the *rillettes*.

Rabbit and Fennel Pie

serves 6–8

1.25 kg ($2\frac{1}{2}$ lb) rabbit pieces

Marinade
4 tablespoons olive oil
juice and zest of half lemon
1 teaspoon fennel seeds
1 teaspoon dried thyme
1 bay leaf
125 g (4 oz) piece of unsmoked
   streaky bacon
olive oil
1 onion, sliced
1.25 kg ($2\frac{1}{2}$ lb) fennel, cut into
   julienne strips
2 tablespoons flour
175 ml (6 fl oz) white wine

600 ml (1 pt) chicken stock
1 tablespoon each of butter and
   flour mashed together, (*beurre
   manié*)
salt and pepper

Biscuit crust
200 g (7 oz) strong white flour
1 teaspoon salt
2 teaspoons baking powder
65 g ($2\frac{1}{2}$ oz) chilled unsalted butter
6 tablespoons of mixed fresh herbs,
   finely chopped
150 ml ($\frac{1}{4}$ pint) buttermilk
1 egg beaten with 1 teaspoon of
   water and a pinch of salt

Mix all the marinade ingredients together, pour over the rabbit pieces and leave for at least 4 hours or overnight. Cut the bacon into lardons and blanch for a few minutes then drain and dry. Fry the bacon in one tablespoon of the oil in a frying pan until brown, remove with a slotted spoon and place in a flameproof casserole. Add the onion to the pan. Stir until the onion has softened then remove to the casserole. Lightly brown a few pieces of rabbit at a time, without wiping off any of the marinade. Add the rabbit to the casserole and any leftover marinade. Stir the fennel into the frying pan adding a bit more oil if necessary, and seasoning with salt and pepper. When they have slightly softened spread them around the rabbit. Sift the flour over the casserole and stir over moderate heat until the flour is distributed. Pour in the wine and boil for a minute then add the stock.

Bring to a simmer, cover, and place in a preheated oven 170°C/ 325°F/gas 3, for about 40 minutes. Strain sauce into a saucepan and turn the rabbit and fennel into a 1.75 litre (3 pint) pie dish. If the sauce is thin thicken it by stirring in the *beurne manié* and simmering the sauce for a few minutes. Taste and adjust the seasoning before pouring over the rabbit. For the biscuit crust, sift the flour, salt and baking powder together, cut in the butter and rub with your fingers until the mixture is crumb-like. Pour in the buttermilk and herbs and stir with a spoon until a soft dough is formed. Roll the dough out on a floured surface and cover the pie, sealing it well around the edge. Glaze with the egg wash and make a few slits for the steam to escape. Bake in a preheated oven 190°C/375°F/gas 5 for about 20 minutes.

Venison Pudding

The rich taste of venison is particularly well suited for puddings and pies.

serves 4–5

For the pastry
115 g (4 oz) self-raising flour
115 g (4 oz) fresh breadcrumbs
a pinch of salt
115 g (4 oz) shredded suet

For the filling
12 pickling onions, peeled
230 g (8 oz) button mushrooms,

2 tablespoons olive oil
570 g (1¼ lb) stewing venison, cubed
1 tablespoon potato or plain flour
½ teaspoon dried thyme
bouquet garni
150 ml (¼ pint) game stock
150 ml (¼ pint) red wine
salt and pepper

Sift the flour into a basin. Mix in the breadcrumbs, salt and suet. Stir in a scant 150 ml (¼ pint) of water, just enough to form a dough. Turn the dough out on to a floured surface and form into a disc. Cover and refrigrate.

Heat the oil in frying pan and sauté the onions and mushrooms until they begin to colour. Remove them from the pan, add the venison and brown on all sides. Stir in the flour and when it is well distributed gradually add the wine and stock, simmer for few minutes, season and set aside to cool.

Grease a 1 litre (2 pint) pudding basin. Roll out three-quarters of

155

the pastry and line the basin. Carefully add the meat filling, vegetables and thyme. Roll out remaining pastry and place on top of basin. Seal the edges. Cover the basin with a sheet of greaseproof paper, pleated in the middle to allow for the pie expanding. Secure the paper with string, then cover the top with a clean tea towel and tie it round the rim of the basin. Bring the ends up over the pudding and tie in a knot. Place basin in large saucepan, pour hot water to come half way up the basin. Cover with a lid and simmer $2\frac{1}{2}$ hours, replenishing the water from time to time if necessary.

Partridge Pudding

The general idea for this recipe is from a Victorian cookbook called *Everybody's Dinner Book* by Lady Constance Howard. The book is ingeniously arranged into menus costing from one shilling to ten. The price for every item on each dish is noted and it is fascinating to read that truffles were only a few pence and a partridge 1s. 6d.

serves 4–5

For the pastry:
115 g (4 oz) self-raising flour
115 g (4 oz) fresh breadcrumbs
115 g (4 oz) shredded fresh suet
$\frac{1}{4}$ teaspoon thyme
$\frac{1}{4}$ teaspoon salt

For the filling:
2 partridge

1 tablespoon oil
1 tablespoon unsalted butter
2 shallots chopped
450 g (1 lb) small mushrooms
1 tablespoon flour
350 g ($\frac{3}{4}$ lb) stewing veal, cubed
300 ml ($\frac{1}{2}$ pint) of partridge or
    game stock

Mix the flour, breadcrumbs, salt and thyme in a bowl. Stir in the suet and just enough water (about 125 ml (scant $\frac{1}{4}$ pint) to make a dough. Knead into a ball, cover, and leave in a cool place while you prepare the filling. Remove as much flesh as possible from the partridge and cut into 1 cm ($\frac{1}{2}$ inch) pieces. Use the carcases for the stock. (Chapter 13) Heat half the oil and butter in a frying pan. Add the shallots, mushrooms, salt and pepper and sauté until the juices start to run, increase the heat and boil away the liquid. Scrape the mushrooms on to a dish. Add another tablespoon of oil and butter to the pan and seal first the veal and then the partridge. Sift the flour over the meat and stir in some of the stock. When the stock has come to a simmer take the pan off the heat and leave to cool.

Grease a 1 litre (2 pt) pudding basin. Roll out three-quarters of the pastry and line the basin. Spoon in the meat, mushrooms and the rest of the stock. Roll out the rest of the pastry to make a lid. Seal the edges with water. Cut a circle of greaseproof paper 5 cm (2 inches) larger all round than the top of the pudding. Pleat the paper so there is room for the pudding to rise slightly and tie in place around the edge of the basin. Cover the pudding with a tea cloth and tie it around the rim of the basin. Bring the ends up over the top and tie into a knot to make a handle. Place the basin in a large saucepan, pour boiling water to come half-way up the basin, cover with a lid and simmer for 2 to $2\frac{1}{2}$ hours. Top up when necessary with boiling water.

Pheasant Terrine with Prunes

This is an excellent terrine to make with left-over pheasant thighs. If the pheasants have been well hung, even the small amount required in the terrine will be enough to give it a delicious pheasant flavour. There is no preliminary cooking and most of the ingredients are blended in a processor so it is quite quick to make.

serves 10–12

350 g (12 oz) prunes
115 ml (scant $\frac{1}{4}$ pint) armagnac or
    brandy
6 pheasant thighs
150 g (5 oz) chicken livers
175 g (6 oz) mushrooms
60 g (2 oz) shallots, peeled and
    quartered

1 clove garlic
30 g (1 oz) parsley leaves
1 teaspoon dried thyme
680 g ($1\frac{1}{2}$ lb) belly of pork, minced
    or chopped very fine
salt and freshly ground black
    pepper

Soak the prunes in the armagnac for at least 48 hours. Bone the thighs and chop the meat coarsely. Place in a processor with the chicken livers, mushrooms, shallots, garlic, parsley leaves, thyme and a good bit of salt and pepper. Blend to a purée. Turn into a bowl and mix with the belly of pork. Add more seasoning and the armagnac from the prunes. Test the seasoning by frying a small patty of the mixture in some oil. Line a 1.7 litre (3 pint) terrine or loaf tin with cling-film.

Place half the mixture in the terrine and layer with the stoned prunes. Cover with the rest of the mixture. Place a piece of foil over the top and set the terrine in a baking pan. Fill the pan with hot water to come half way of the side of the terrine and bake in a preheated oven 180°C/350°F/gas 4 for $1\frac{1}{4}$–$1\frac{1}{2}$ hours. Top up the water in the bain-marie as necessary. Remove from the oven and cool. The terrine can be weighted if you want a firmer texture and shape. Keep refrigerated and leave for 24 hours before serving.

Game Terrine

350 g (12 oz) boned raw game meat such as partridge, pheasant or pigeon
230 g ($\frac{1}{2}$ lb) lean veal, diced
230 g ($\frac{1}{2}$ lb) fresh pork fat (from the back), diced
4 tablespoons madeira
6 juniper berries, crushed
5 peppercorns, crushed

small clove of garlic, very finely chopped
350 g (12 oz) sliced green streaky bacon, rind removed
450 g (1 lb) minced pork, half lean and half fat
a pinch of allspice
1 egg
salt

Cut about half of the game meat into strips. Mix the strips with the diced veal and pork fat then mix in the madeira, juniper berries, peppercorns, garlic, and salt. Cover and marinate for at least 2 hours.

Mince the remaining game meat with one slice of bacon. Turn into a large bowl and mix with the minced pork. Drain the marinade into the bowl, add the egg, allspice and season well with salt and pepper. Line a 1.5 litre ($2\frac{1}{2}$ pint) terrine mould with bacon, saving 2 slices for the top. Spread a quarter of the minced meat into the bottom of the terrine, cover with about one-third of the meat strips. Repeat twice more ending with the last of the minced meat, and topping with the reserved bacon. Cover the terrine with foil and then the lid, making it as air-tight as possible. Set the terrine in a roasting tin and fill with hot water. Place in a preheated oven 180°C/350°F/gas 4 for $1\frac{1}{2}$ hours. Refrigrate when cool. The terrine should be left for 2 days to allow the flavours to mellow, but it will keep for up to one week in the refrigerator or can be frozen.

Pigeon and Mincemeat Pie

An adapted version of a recipe from *The Sunday Times* created by the London Chef Alastair Little.

serves 4

2 wood pigeons
250 g (8 oz) good sausage
　meat
2 eggs

150 g ($4\frac{1}{2}$ oz) mincemeat (as for
　mince pies)
200 g (7 oz) puff pastry
salt and pepper

Remove the breasts from the pigeons and peel off the skin. The remaining pigeon carcases can be used for a delicious stock. Place the breasts between cling-film and flatten slightly using a rolling pin. Season lightly with salt and pepper. Mix the sausage meat, mincemeat and one egg together. Place half the mixture in a 22 cm ($8\frac{1}{2}$ in) pie dish about 4 cm ($1\frac{1}{2}$ in) deep. Place the breasts in a radial fashion over the top and cover with the remaining sausage mixture. Whisk the second egg with a pinch of salt. Roll out the pastry, cover the pie and seal the edge with the egg wash. Decorate the top with pastry leaves made from the pastry scraps. Glaze the pastry and refrigerate until ready to bake. Bake in an oven preheated to 200°C/400°F/gas 6 for 10 minutes then reduce the oven to 180°C/350°F/gas 4 and bake for a further 25 minutes. Serve hot.

———— •●• ————

Venison Pâté en Crôute with Spinach

It takes no particular skill to produce this most delicious pâté and it is handsome enough to adorn Fauchon's window in the Place de la Madeleine

serves 8–10

For the pastry
450 g (1 lb) plain flour
2 teaspoons salt
65 g (2½ oz) lard
140 g (4½ oz) unsalted butter
1 egg
4 tablespoons iced water
small egg beaten with a pinch of salt

For the filling
350 g (12 oz) boneless venison steak
4 tablespoons brandy
2 crushed juniper berries
2 shallots, chopped very fine

1 tablespoon oil
450 g (1 lb) shoulder or belly of pork, minced
2 eggs, beaten
½ teaspoon ground allspice
½ teaspoon dried thyme
120 g (4 oz) mild cure smoked streaky bacon
120 g (4 oz) raw young spinach leaves, stalks removed
175 g (6 oz) cooked sliced ham
8 tablespoons jellied chicken stock or aspic
salt and freshly ground black pepper

Sift the flour and salt into a mixing bowl. Cut the lard and butter in pea-size pieces and rub into the flour. Add the beaten egg and water and mix to a dough. Form the dough into a flat rectangular shape, cover in cling-film and refrigerate while you prepare the filling.

Cut the venison into thin slices, mix with the brandy and juniper berries and leave to marinate for at least one hour.

Heat the oil in a small saucepan, add the shallot and stir over low heat until it softens. Turn into a large bowl. Add the minced pork, eggs, allspice, thyme, salt and pepper and the drained brandy from the venison. Roll ¾ of the pastry out and line a 26 cm (11 in) hinged raised pie tin. Arrange alternate layers of the mince, venison, bacon, spinach and ham. You may prefer to use all the spinach to make one layer in the middle of the other ingredients. It may seem a lot of spinach but it will cook down to quite a thin stripe. Roll out the remaining pastry and cover the top, sealing the edges with water. Pierce 2 holes on the top to allow the steam to escape. Place a funnel of foil in each hole to keep them open. Use the scraps of leftover pastry to make decorations for the top. Glaze with the beaten egg and bake in a preheated oven 180°C/350°F/gas 4 for one hour. Reduce the temperature to 170°C/325°F/gas 3 and cook a further hour, covering the top with foil if it threatens to become too dark. Leave to cool for several hours or overnight then pour the melted but cool stock through the holes. Remove from the tin, wrap in foil and refrigerate for at least several hours before slicing and serving.

Terrine of Salmon, Herbs and Cucumber

serves 6–8

1 kg (2¼ lb) tailpiece of salmon
1.25 kg (3 lb) bones, heads from white fish and salmon
225 ml (scant ½ pint) dry white wine
1 small carrot, sliced
1 onion, sliced
1 bunch of parsley
2 teaspoons gelatine
1 good bunch of chives

1 good bunch of chervil
1 small bunch of tarragon
half a cucumber, peeled and thinly sliced
salt and pepper

for the sauce
450 ml (¾ pint) mayonnaise
1 tablespoon green peppercorns
salt, pepper and lemon juice

Brush a piece of foil with oil, season the salmon, place on the foil and twist the edges together to make a baggy but tightly closed parcel. Place the parcel in a saucepan and add cold water to within 2.5 cm (1 inch) of the top. Bring the water to the boil, let it give 4 or 5 good bubblings then cover, remove from the heat but leave the fish in the water to cool.

Remove the bones and skin from the salmon and put them in a saucepan along with the other fish bones, carrot, onion, stalks from the parsley and wine. Add just enough water to barely cover and simmer for 25 minutes. Strain then boil rapidly to reduce to 750 ml (1¼ pints).

Wash and dry the herbs. Divide all the herbs in half and place half in a sieve. Pour boiling water over the herbs, drain and purée in a blender for the sauce. Chop the remaining herbs and mix with the flaked salmon. Season with salt and pepper. Place the gelatine in a small cup with 1 tablespoon of cold water. Leave to soften then place the cup in simmering water until the gelatine has dissolved. Mix the gelatine with the reduced stock.

161

Pour a thin layer of stock in the bottom of a soufflé dish and refrigerate until it is nearly set. Place slices of cucumber over this and spoon a little stock over the cucumber. Refrigerate for a few minutes. Meanwhile mix the remaining stock into the salmon and season if necessary. Spoon the salmon over the cucumber and refrigerate until set.

Add the puréed herbs and green peppercorns to the mayonnaise and season. Place the soufflé dish in boiling water for a minute or two before turning out and serving.

TROUT AND
SALMON

Trout and Salmon

BRITISH TROUT occur in two types. The non-migratory brown trout and the migratory sea trout. The variations in the brown or common trout are numerous and caused by the differing waters and feeding habits. Brown trout with pink flesh weighing nearly forty pounds have been caught in deep lakes in Scotland and Wales. Trout living in fast flowing moorland streams may only weigh half a pound and have white flesh.

The sea trout (or salmon trout) spends its early life in a river but between the ages of one and three years old it goes down to the open sea. Until then it is identical with the brown trout but in the sea it grows much faster and returns to the river to spawn, often it seems with a common trout. While in the sea it takes on a silvery colour and its flesh becomes pinkish.

The rainbow trout originated in California but now occurs world-wide. It is very similar to the brown trout but differs in colouring with a reddish purple band along its flank. It is often chosen for farming because of its hardiness.

The salmon belongs to the salmonidae family as does the trout. Most types of salmon are primarily sea fish; Western European and North American salmon living their sea lives in the waters of Greenland. All salmon spawn in fresh water and each fish, male and female, returns to the waters in which they were born. This may involve tremendous journeys ending in battles to overcome river currents and obstacles. These journeys take place in Spring, Summer and Autumn. Spawning occurs in the Autumn. The Pacific salmon dies after spawning but the Atlantic salmon may live to spawn again. They are called 'kelts' when they have spawned. The eggs are laid in hollows made in sand or gravel by the female who then covers them. They incubate for some five weeks and then spend some two years or more in the fresh water, being then known as 'smolts'. They then seek the sea where they live for one to three years before returning to the fresh water stream of their birth.

Farmed trout and salmon are widely available. Some large farmed pink-fleshed trout are called salmon trout at the fishmonger's and should not be confused with the wild salmon trout or sea trout. There is no question that, adequate though some farmed fish may be, a fresh game fish with its fine flavour and firm texture is an altogether different beast.

Char, along with trout, grayling, sea trout and whitefish belong to the same family as the salmon. The char is found in arctic seas but was also found in isolated waters in Scotland and Ireland. Char were plentiful in the eighteenth and nineteenth centuries in Lake Windermere and were made into potted char, a delicacy sold in attractive round shallow pottery decorated with fish. Other varieties of char include the *Omble chevalier* in France and the Swiss Alps, and the lake and brook trout of North America.

In the 1890s and earlier whitebait netted in the Thames, were fried up and served in many river taverns. This was often preceded by a light fish stew called Water Souchy (from the Dutch *waterzootje*) made from the other odd fish netted along with the whitebait. On grand occasions, such as the dinners marking the recess of summer parliament, whitebait dinners were the fashion but the Water Souchy was upgraded and made with the esteemed char.

Any of the trout recipes can be used for char and the fresher the fish the better the results.

———— •••• ————

Potted Char

serves 6

3 char of average trout size	60 g (2 oz) melted butter
150 ml ($\frac{1}{4}$ pint) white wine	$\frac{1}{4}$ teaspoon ground mace
bayleaf	pinch of ginger
a few parsley stalks	salt and pepper

Preheat the oven to 190°C/375°F/gas 5. Place fish in one layer in a shallow oven dish. Add the wine, bay leaf and parsley stalks, cover, and bake for 25–30 minutes. Remove the flesh from the fish and mix with the butter. Reduce the pan juices to a few tablespoons and add to the fish. Season with mace, ginger, salt and pepper. Chill for 24 hours before serving. Serve with brown toast. The paste will keep for several days if sealed with melted butter.

Trout Fillets with Pine Kernels

Trout fillets are coated in chopped pine nuts and briefly sautéed.

serves 4

8 trout fillets, skinned
8 tablespoons pine kernels
salt and pepper

1 oz (25 g) butter
2 tablespoons oil
1 lemon cut into wedges

Rub your finger against the grain the of the fillets to find any remaining bones and remove these with tweezers. Season lightly with salt and pepper. Chop the pine nuts very fine and coat the fillets on both sides with a good layer of the nuts. Heat the oil and butter in a frying pan and sauté the fillets for about 2–3 minutes each side. Carefully remove them to individual warmed plates. They are thin and need to be handled gently to keep them from breaking. Serve with a wedge of lemon.

Steamed Trout Fillets
with Chive Sauce

Other fish fillets can be used for this recipe and the stuffing can also be varied. Matchsticks of fennel, softened first in a bit of oil or butter, are a good alternative and mixed chopped herbs with breadcrumbs and butter another.

serves 6

2 shallots, very finely chopped
1 tablespoon oil
175 g (6 oz) mushrooms, finely
   chopped
squeeze of lemon juice
salt and pepper
8 large lettuce leaves
6 large pink trout fillets, skinned

For the sauce;
15 g ($\frac{1}{2}$ oz/1 tablespoon) unsalted
   butter
150 g ($\frac{1}{4}$ pint) white wine
150 g ($\frac{1}{4}$ pint) fish stock (chapter 13)
150 g ($\frac{1}{4}$ pint) double cream
3 tablespoons finely chopped chives
salt and pepper.

Sweat halt the shallots in the oil. Add the mushrooms, lemon juice, salt and pepper. Sauté until the mushrooms give off their juices, then boil hard until all the juices have evaporated.

Blanch the lettuce by placing in a colander and pouring boiling water over them. Drain on tea towels.

Trim the fillets and remove any bones with tweezers. By running your finger against the grain of the flesh, you can feel where they are. Pat the fillets dry and season. Place a spoonful of mushrooms on the fillet and roll up. Wrap in a lettuce leaf, and place seam-down in a steaming basket. Steam for 20 minutes.

For the sauce, sweat the remaining shallot in the butter, pour in the wine and reduce by half. Add the fish stock and reduce then add the cream and simmer until it thickens slightly. Stir in the chives and season. Serve poured over the fish parcels.

Note: The fish parcels can be assembled ahead of time and the sauce made in advance.

Trout and Sole Seviche

Seviche is a South American way of preparing fish by marinating it in lime or lemon juice. The acidity of the juice causes the flesh to become opaque and 'cooks' it. Any fresh fish can be used for seviche but this combination of pink trout and white sole is particularly attractive.

serves 6

450 g (1 lb) trout fillets
450 g (1 lb) sole fillets, skinned
150 ml ($\frac{1}{4}$ pint) lime juice
$\frac{1}{2}$ red onion or 6 spring onions, sliced very fine
1 teaspoon freshly ground black pepper
2 tablespoons finely chopped coriander leaves

2 tablespoons olive oil
$1\frac{1}{2}$ teaspoons salt
3 tomatoes, skinned, seeded and chopped
1 tablespoon, very finely chopped parsley
salad leaves

Remove any remaining bones from the fillets with tweezers, then cut the fillets into thin slices. Mix the lime juice, onion, pepper, coriander and salt together, then pour over the fish. Cover and refrigerate for at least 3 hours. Before serving mix the fish with the tomatoes and serve on the salad leaves garnished with fresh parsley.

Trout à la Meunière

Although this is one of the best known methods of cooking trout it is also one of the best. If the trout are fresh and the cooking done carefully the skin should be deliciously crisp and the flesh tender and moist.

serves 4

4 fresh trout, cleaned
seasoned flour
85 g (3 oz) unsalted butter
1 tablespoon oil

50 g (2 oz) slivered almonds
(optional)
juice of $\frac{1}{2}$ lemon

Roll each trout in seasoned flour, shaking them to remove the excess. Heat 60 g (2 oz) of butter with the oil in a frying pan large enough to hold the fish in one layer. When the butter is frothy add the fish. Fry the trout for about 5 minutes on one side, turn carefully and fry the second side for 5 minutes. Remove the fish to heated plates. Add the remaining butter to the pan and brown the almonds if you are using them. Remove the pan from the heat, add the lemon juice and spoon both almonds and juices over the fish.

Variation: Cook the trout *à la meunière* but omit the almond and lemon. Cook 100 g (3½ oz) of butter to a nut-brown colour, immediately add 30 g (1 oz) of very fine white breadcrumbs, and cook until crumbs are golden. Sprinkle over the fish with a little lemon juice and chopped parsley.

Trout Fillets with Ginger and Lime

serves 6

12 trout fillets
melted butter
18 thin slices of fresh ginger
18 thin slices of stem ginger,
  preserved in syrup

juice of 3 limes
salt and pepper
12 tablespoons of white wine

Cut out 12 pieces of foil large enough to wrap a trout fillet. Brush a little butter in the centre of each piece of foil. Season the fish well and set it skin-side down on the foil. Divide the ginger and lime juice over the fillets. Make a slightly roomy but tightly sealed package with the foil and leave in a cool place for several hours. Preheat the oven to 190°C/375°F/gas 5. Bake the parcels for 8 minutes.

Cold Salmon with Sorrel and Pear Sauce

serves 6

1 kg–1.25 kg (2½–2¾ lb) centre cut
of salmon
milk
bay leaf
15 g (½ oz) unsalted butter
2 ripe pears

large handful of sorrel leaves,
centre stalks removed
150 ml (¼ pint) whipped cream
salt and pepper

Season the salmon with salt and pepper and set it in a saucepan large enough for it to sit comfortably in. Cover with cold milk. Add a bay leaf and bring slowly to the boil. Allow the milk to give a few strong bubbles, cover and remove the pan from the heat. Leave the fish in the covered pan until the liquid has cooled to lukewarm. Drain the salmon and cool. Save the cooking liquid for soup.

Peel, core and slice the pear. Heat the butter in a small saucepan, add the pear and cook gently to soften. Chop the sorrel and add to the pear with a pinch of salt. When the sorrel has wilted purée the mixture in a blender. Once the purée is cool fold in the cream and serve with the cold salmon.

Note: If you wish to serve the salmon hot reduce the heat after the first strong bubblings and simmer the fish for 5 minutes. Turn off the heat and leave the fish for 10 minutes in the milk by which time the fish should be just cooked through. Use some of the liquid to make a velouté sauce to serve with the fish.

Poached Salmon with Warm Vinaigrette

serves 6

For the poaching liquid
900 ml (1½ pints) dry white wine
8 tablespoons white wine vinegar
½ carrot, sliced
½ small onion, peeled and sliced
½ celery stalk, sliced
¼ tomato, coarsely chopped
pinch of thyme
2 teaspoons salt
½ bay leaf
12 peppercorns
6 × 300 g (10 oz) salmon steaks

For the vinaigrette
3-4 tablespoons each of sherry and
    red wine vinegar
8 tablespoons olive oil
8 tablespoons sunflower oil
1 teaspoon dijon mustard
2 tablespoons shallots, very finely
    chopped
3 tablespoons mixed fresh herbs,
    such as chives, tarragon or chervil
salt and freshly ground black
    pepper

Combine 2½ quarts of cold water with poaching ingredients in an non-aluminium stockpot. Cover and bring to the boil, simmer for 15 minutes then strain into a pan large enough to hold fish in one layer. Cool to room temperature.

Place fish in liquid and bring to a boil, lower heat and simmer for 5 minutes. Remove from heat and leave fish in hot court-bouillon for 10 minutes before serving. Meanwhile make the vinaigrette, using the smaller amount of vinegar and leaving out the herbs. Set over low heat until warm to the touch. Add extra vinegar if needed. Just before serving stir in the herbs and serve spooned over the fish.

Note: If serving fish at room temperature; place the fish in court-bouillon and bring to a boil. Let it bubble once or twice quite fiercely, then cover, remove from the heat and allow fish to cool to tepid in the liquid.

Papillotes of Salmon with Chervil Butter

Fish steaks baked in papillotes keep beautifully moist and imbibe the herb flavours they are sealed with.

serves 6

6 170 g (6 oz) each thick salmon steaks
60 g (2 oz) softened butter
2 tablespoons fresh finely chopped chervil

salt and freshly ground black pepper
Oil

Mash the butter and chervil together and season well with salt and pepper. Wrap in cling-film and refrigerate until firm if preparing in advance.

Cut 6 heart-shapes from greaseproof paper large enough to contain a steak when folded in half. Oil one half of the paper and place a well seasoned steak on it. Divide the butter into 6 parts and place on top of the fish. Seal the parcels by crimping the edges, to make a tightly sealed but roomy package. (Foil can be used.) Preheat the oven to 190°C/375°F/gas 5 and bake parcels for 10–12 minutes. Do not overcook.

Salmon and Shrimp Ravioli

Won-ton wrappers (available in Oriental food stores) are small squares of paper-thin fresh pasta that can be bought in stacks all ready for stuffing. This eliminates rolling out sheets of dough and means the effort of creating your own ravioli at home is minimal.

serves 6 as a first course

For the filling
230 g ($\frac{1}{2}$ lb) boned and skinned
    fresh salmon fillet
340 g (12 oz) prawns
2 shallots, very finely chopped
2 tablespoons butter
2 teaspoons fresh mint
salt and pepper
72 won-ton wrappers
yolk of one egg mixed with 2
    tablespoons of water

For the sauce
2 shallots, finely chopped
2 tablespoons white wine vinegar
4 tablespoons white wine
6 tablespoons double cream
140 g (5 oz) cold butter
2 teaspoons of very finely chopped
    fresh mint
salt and pepper

Chop the salmon and prawns very fine. Sweat the shallots in the butter until soft. Stir in the fish and sauté for about 1 minute. Remove from the heat and add the mint, salt and pepper. Place a teaspoon of the fish in the centre of a won-ton square. Brush the egg wash around the edge and place another wrapper over the top, pressing around the edge to seal. Either cut into rounds with a pastry cutter or use a pastry wheel to make a fluted edge around the sides of the square. Continue until all the filling is used. Spread the ravioli on a flour-dusted cloth set on a tray and keep in a cool place (not the refrigerator) until ready to use. They can be made up to 4–5 hours in advance.

Fill a large sauté pan or saucepan with boiling salted water. Slide about a quarter of the ravioli into the boiling water and simmer gently for 2–3 minutes. Remove with a slotted spoon and keep warm while you poach the rest.

Place the shallots, white wine vinegar and wine in a saucepan and reduce to 2 tablespoons. Add the cream and simmer for one minute. Cut the butter into small pieces and whisk them into the sauce, a few at a time, on and off the heat so the butter thickens the sauce rather than melts into it. Season with salt and pepper. Place several ravioli on individual plates, spoon some sauce over the top and decorate with a tiny pinch of mint.

Salmon en Croûte with Spinach and Sorrel Stuffing

A good sized piece of salmon, boned and skinned, is stuffed, wrapped in several sheets of buttered filo pastry and baked. The salmon stays beautifully moist and is easy to serve in attractive slices.

serves 8

1 kg (2¼ lb) centre piece of salmon, boned and skinned
50 g (2 oz) unsalted butter
small bunch spring onions, chopped fine
1 clove garlic, chopped fine
150 g (5 oz) chopped, cooked fresh spinach
100 g (3½ oz) chopped, cooked fresh sorrel (if unavailable use more spinach)
50 g (2 oz) soft brown breadcrumbs
4 tablespoons whipping cream
lemon juice if not using sorrel
6 sheets of filo pastry
40 g (1½ oz) melted butter
salt and freshly ground black pepper

Run your fingers against the grain of the salmon flesh to find any remaining bones. Pull them out with tweezers or a potato peeler. Season both sides of the salmon with salt and pepper.

Melt the butter and sauté the garlic and spring onions until soft but not coloured. Tip in the spinach and sorrel and stir over high heat to evaporate most of the moisture. Off the heat, stir in the breadcrumbs, cream and season with salt and pepper.

Spread the mixture along the inside of one half of the salmon and then place the other half on top. Unroll the filo leaves and brush 6 slices, one at a time, with the melted butter, stacking them in a pile as you go.

Place a baking sheet in the centre of the oven and preheat to 190°C/375°F/gas 5. Place the salmon in the centre of the filo and make a parcel, folding the edges under the brushing with butter. Place on a baking sheet and set on the hot oven sheet. Bake for 25 minutes. Rest for 5 minutes before serving. Cut into 8 slices with a sharp serrated knife using a sawing motion. This should produce neat slices.

Sumptuous Salmon Cakes

These are – bar none – the best fish cakes I have ever tasted.

serves 6

750 g (1½ lbs) fresh salmon fillet
85 g (3 oz) fresh bread crumbs
300 ml (½ pint) double cream
1 tablespoon fresh tarragon or 2
   tablespoons of dill, finely
   chopped

salt and freshly ground black
   pepper
a good dash of tabasco
5 tablespoons oil
1 lemon cut into wedges

Chop the salmon into 1 cm (½ inch) dice. Place in a bowl and add half the bread crumbs. Stir in the cream and season well with the tarragon, tabasco, salt and pepper. Form into 6 cakes and coat in the remaining crumbs. Refrigerate for 30 minutes. Before serving, heat the oil in a frying pan and sauté for about 4 minutes each side. Serve piping hot with the lemon wedges.

OTHER FISH

Other Fish

Carp Hungarian Style

If your carp has been fished from the muddy depths of a pond or river it is prudent to soak it in water with added vinegar – about 4 pints of water to 6 tablespoons of vinegar. This should be done after the fish is cleaned and the gall sac at the base of the head removed. Most of the carp one is likely to encounter at the fishmonger will have been farmed to meet the needs of the Chinese and Jewish communities.

serves 4

$1\frac{1}{2}$ kg (3 lb) carp
120 g (4 oz) streaky bacon
2 tablespoons olive oil
1 large onion, finely chopped
3 green peppers, cored, seeded
   and sliced

230 g ($\frac{1}{2}$ lb) tomatoes, peeled,
   seeded and cubed
paprika
300 ml ($\frac{1}{2}$ pint) soured cream
25 g (1 oz) butter
salt

Clean and scale the fish. Chop the bacon and fry it until it starts to turn crisp. Drain off the fat and add the oil and onions. Sweat the onions until they are transparent. Add 1 teaspoon of paprika, the tomatoes and the sliced peppers. Season with salt and simmer for 10 minutes, until the peppers are half-cooked. Place the fish in an oiled baking dish. Spoon the pepper mixture over the fish and pour the soured cream on top. Dot with butter and bake in a preheated oven 180°C/350°F/gas 4 for 30–35 minutes.

——— •••• ———

Sweet and Sour Steamed Carp

serves 2–3

680 g (1½ lb) carp, cleaned
2 tablespoons olive oil
2 tablespoons groundnut oil
1 chilli pepper, seeded and cut
    into fine shreds
small piece of root ginger, sliced
6 spring onions, cut diagonally into
    5 cm (2 inch) pieces

3 tablespoons light soy sauce
3 tablespoons wine vinegar
1 tablespoon tomato purée
juice of half a small orange
1 tablespoon brown sugar
1 tablespoon cornflour

Rub the fish inside and out with salt and olive oil. Leave for 45 minutes before steaming the fish over boiling water for 15 minutes.

Heat the groundnut oil in a wok or frying pan. Add the chilli pepper, ginger and spring onion and stir for one minute. Add the soy sauce, vinegar, tomato purée, orange juice and sugar and cook for a further 8 minutes. Dissolve the arrowroot in 3 tablespoons of cold water, add to the ingredients and stir until the mixture thickens slightly. Pour the sauce over the fish and serve.

————— •●• —————

Quenelles de Brochet

One of the best reasons for having a food processor is the ease with which you can make delicate mousselines. Quenelles or mousse in any form can be made with a minimum of effort. The lightness of the mousse is determined by the amount of cream it will hold. By keeping all the ingredients very cold, more cream can be incorporated and the resulting quenelles will be delicate and meltingly tender.

serves 4

For the quenelles
350 g (12 oz) skinned and boned
fillets of pike
1 teaspoon salt
1 whole egg
1 egg white
pinch of white pepper
grating of nutmeg
150 ml ($\frac{1}{2}$ pint) double cream

For the sauce
2 teaspoons unsalted butter
1 shallot, very finely chopped
140 g (5 oz) peeled prawns,
   chopped
125 ml (scant $\frac{1}{4}$ pint) white wine
250 ml (scant $\frac{1}{2}$ pint) fish stock
1 tablespoon dry vermonth
3 tablespoons double cream
30 g (1 oz) butter, cut into
   small pieces
salt and pepper

Place the bowl of a food processor in the freezer. Keep fish and cream very cold.

For the sauce, soften the shallot and prawns in the butter, stirring over gentle heat. Add the white wine and stock and reduce by half. Purée in a blender and work through a fine sieve into a clean saucepan. Add the vermonth and cream and season. Set aside.

Cut the fish into pieces and check carefully for any remaining bones. Purée in the cold processor bowl for a full 4–5 minutes. Add the salt and purée again. Slowly pour in the eggs and spices and blend until very smooth. Scrape down the sides from time to time. With the machine running, add the cream very slowly and stop the moment it is well blended. Do not overmix. Return the container to the refrigerator for 1 hour.

Shape the mousseline into quenelles, using two spoons dipped in cold water. Heap the mixture on one spoon, invert it onto the second spoon and slide into a buttered roasting tin or large pan. Add enough hot water to cover the quenelle, add some salt and bring to a simmer. Poach at a bare simmer for 10 minutes. The water should just quiver and not be bubbling. Remove with a slotted spoon and arrange on heated serving plates. Reheat the sauce and stir in the butter, bit by bit, off and on the heat so the butter thickens the sauce rather than melts into it. Spoon some sauce over the quenelles and serve at once.

Note: Delicious fish quenelles can be made using salmon, sole or brill. The quenelles can be prepared a day in advance. Cover and store in one layer in the refrigerator. Before serving return the quenelles to a buttered roasting tin. Cover with hot water and poach for 5–8 minutes or until just heated through.

Perch

In France and Italy perch is considered one of the best of the fresh water fish. In northern Italy it is often served filleted coated in bread-crumbs and egg and fried. In France the larger perch are stuffed and baked, and the smaller ones fried. The flesh is firmer than that of trout but recipes for both fish can be used interchangeably. If perch or indeed carp are not pristine fresh they can be difficult to scale. One solution is to plunge the fish in boiling water for a few seconds and remove scales and skin.

Baked Perch Stuffed with Mushrooms

serves 6

1.5 kg (3.5 lb) perch, cleaned and scaled
3 shallots, finely chopped
60 g (2 oz) unsalted butter
170 g (7 oz) chopped mushrooms
squeeze of lemon juice
5 tablespoons of breadcrumbs

2 tablespoons finely chopped parsley
2 tablespoons cream
salt and pepper
melted butter
150 ml ($\frac{1}{4}$ pint) white wine

Using a frying pan, sweat about half the shallots in the butter until they have softened. Add the mushrooms, salt, pepper and lemon juice. Sauté the mushrooms until they give off their own moisture, raise the heat and boil most of this away. Scrape into a bowl and mix

with the breadcrumbs and cream, half the parsley and more seasoning. Stuff the fish with this mixture. Butter a baking dish, scatter the
remaining shallots and parsley over the butter and lay the fish on top.
Brush the fish with melted butter and bake in a preheated oven,
200°C/400°F/gas 6, about 15 minutes. Pour over the wine and bake
for a further 10 minutes. Serve with boiled new potatoes.

Baked Perch with Herb Crust

serves 4

4 good sized fillets of perch,
   skinned
5 tablespoons extra virgin olive oil
juice of half a lemon
3 tablespoons of mixed fresh herbs
   such as chives, tarragon, basil,
   chervil and parsley, very finely
   chopped

50 g (2 oz) breadcrumbs
salt and freshly ground black
   pepper

Preheat the oven to 230°C/450°F/gas 8. Place the fish in an oven dish
large enough for them to fit in one layer. Marinate them in the lemon
juice, 1 tablespoon of the oil, 1 tablespoon of the herb mixture and
freshly ground black pepper for 30 minutes. Meanwhile mix the
breadcrumbs, oil and remaining herbs together and season with salt
and pepper. Cover the fillets with a good layer of the mixture, pressing it down to make a firm crust. Bake at the top of the oven,
uncovered, for about 10 minutes for thick fillets, and 8 minutes for
thinner ones.

———— •●• ————

Blackened Swordfish

Odette Bery is the chef/owner of Boston's Another Season restaurant. Her charming restaurant enjoys a reputation for its innovative yet fresh tasting food. This is a recipe from her book *Another Season Cookbook*. Odette suggests serving the fish with a tossed green salad and warm cornbread.

serves 4

4 × 140 g (5 oz) swordfish steaks
1 cm ($\frac{1}{2}$ in) thick
2 teaspoons fennel seeds
1 tablespoon whole black
peppercorns
2 teaspoons dried thyme

$\frac{1}{2}$ teaspoon salt
1 teaspoon dried basil
$\frac{1}{4}$ teaspoon cayenne pepper
2 tablespoons vegetable oil
4 tablespoons unsalted butter

Place the fennel seed and black peppercorns in a very dry blender (I use a coffee grinder) and blend fine. Add the thyme, salt, basil and cayenne and blend for 30 seconds until fairly fine, but not a powder. Just before serving brush each fish steak lavishly with oil. Melt the butter in a large cast-iron or heavy sauté pan until it gently bubbles. At the same time, lightly coat the fish with spices. Sauté the fillets over medium heat until they are a light golden brown, about 4–5 minutes. Turn them over and cook the second side for another 4–5 minutes. Serve immediately.

Note: If you wish to take up Odette's suggestion, here is her excellent recipe for cornbread: 85 g (3 oz) fresh corn kernels, (Scrape down the sides of a fresh ear of corn with a knife) 140 g (5 oz) yellow cornmeal, 120 g ($4\frac{1}{2}$ oz) plain flour, 1 tablespoon baking powder, 1 tablespoon sugar, 2 teaspoons salt, 2 large eggs, 175 ml ($\frac{1}{3}$ pint) milk, 120 g (4 oz) melted unsalted butter at room temperature. Preheat oven to 190°C/375°F/gas 5. Butter a 20 cm (8 × 8 × 2 inch) square pan. Process corn kernels to a medium coarse purée. Place all the dry ingredients in a bowl, make a well in the centre and pour in the puréed corn, eggs, milk, and butter. Whisk from the centre until the mixture is smooth. Pour the batter into the pan and bake for 30–35 minutes. Leave bread in pan to cool slightly. Serve warm with unsalted butter.

Grilled Swordfish with Mushroom and Coriander Sauce

serves 6

6 × 170 g (6 oz) swordfish steaks

For the marinade:
juice of one lime
juice of half a lime
4 tablespoons olive oil
1 tablespoon mixed chives and
    coriander, chopped fine

For the sauce
1 clove garlic, finely chopped
230 g (8 oz) mushrooms

2 tablespoons extra virgin olive oil
squeeze of lime juice
75 g (3 oz) fresh coriander leaves
3 tablespoons pine nuts
30 g (1 oz) breadcrumbs
few tablespoons of fish or
    chicken stock
salt and pepper
2 avocados, sliced
2 tomatoes, skinned, seeded
    and sliced

Marinate the fish for 30 minutes to one hour.

Meanwhile make the sauce; sweat the garlic in a few tablespoons of oil without allowing it to colour. Stir in the sliced mushrooms, season with salt, pepper and lime juice and simmer until the mushrooms are tender. Place the mushrooms in a blender with the chopped coriander leaves, pine nuts and olive oil and blend. Add the breadcrumbs, salt and pepper and enough fish or chicken stock to make a thick purée.

Grill the fish for a few minutes each side. Place the fish on heated plates and decorate with a fan shape of alternate avocado and tomato slices and a small mound of the purée.

Note: this sauce is also delicious with most game.

—— •●• ——

Steamed Pike with Sorrel Sauce

Our son, when quite a small boy, spent many hours lying on his stomach on a bridge that spans the Windrush. He kept his head well back from the edge of the river but held tight to a noose that he had made from thin wire. We were sceptical indeed when he told us that he was going to snare a pike and amazed when he did just that. Could he have read Walton's *Compleat Angler*? It became a favourite summer occupation for several years and I had the pleasure of preparing a good number of fresh pike of different sizes.

serves 6

1.25 kg (3 lb) pike, cleaned and
    scaled

For the court-bouillon
1 litre ($1\frac{3}{4}$ pints) water
$\frac{1}{2}$ litre (1 pint) dry white wine
1 carrot, sliced
1 leek, sliced
bouquet garni
2 teaspoons salt
1 teaspoon peppercorns

For the sauce
1 shallot, very finely chopped
250 ml (scant $\frac{1}{2}$ pint) fish stock
2 tablespoons white wine
150 ml ($\frac{1}{4}$ pint) double cream
60 g (2 oz) sorrel leaves, centre vein
    and stalks removed
salt and pepper

Simmer the court-bouillon ingredients for 30 minutes. Place the fish on the strainer of a fish kettle, pour over the court-bouillon, cover and simmer until the fish is cooked, about 20 minutes.

Meanwhile place shallot, white wine and fish stock in a saucepan and reduce by half, add cream and bring to a simmer. Pour into a blender and add the sorrel. Purée then return to the pan. Adjust the seasoning and serve with the fish.

———— ••• ————

Grilled Swordfish with Herb Mayonnaise

serves 6

6 × 200 g (7 oz) swordfish steaks
about $2\frac{1}{2}$ cm (1 in) thick
4 tablespoons olive oil
2 tablespoons mixed fresh herbs,
very finely chopped

250 ml (scant $\frac{1}{2}$ pint) home-made
mayonnaise
3 anchovy fillets, soaked in milk
then finely chopped

Mix 1 tablespoon of the herbs with the olive oil and rub over the fish. Leave to marinate for 30 minutes. Mix the remaining herbs and anchovies into the mayonnaise. Preheat the grill. Grill the swordfish for 4–5 minutes on one side. Turn the fish over and grill for 3 minutes, smear a coating of mayonnaise on the fish and grill until the mayonnaise becomes lightly browned. Serve with the remaining mayonnaise passed separately.

Variation: Make a little fresh tomato and basil sauce by simmering 3 skinned, seeded and chopped tomatoes with 1 tablespoon of olive oil and several shredded basil leaves. When the tomatoes thicken, cool slightly and fold in a few tablespoons of whipped cream. After the second side of the fish is grilled lightly, coat with the tomato sauce and grill until lightly browned. Serve immediately.

Swordfish Kebabs

serves 6

1.25 kg (3 lb) swordfish or shark
steaks
150 ml ($\frac{1}{4}$ pint) olive oil
juice of one lemon
2 tablespoons fresh basil or 3 sprigs
of thyme
1 yellow pepper

1 green pepper
4 tomatoes, skinned, seeded and
quartered
2 mild red onions, peeled and cut
into wedges (optional)
salt and pepper

Mix together the olive oil, lemon juice, herb, salt and pepper. Cut the fish into good sized cubes and marinate for 15–20 minutes.

Meanwhile grill the peppers until the skins are charred. Peel, seed

187

and cut the flesh into thick strips. Alternate pieces of tomato, pepper, onion if you are using it and fish on skewers. Grill for 8–10 minutes, turning the skewers half-way through the cooking time. Serve with some of the marinade poured over or with a wedge of lemon.

Swordfish with Pesto

serves 4

4 fresh swordfish steaks,
  2 cm ($\frac{3}{4}$ inch) thick
60 g (2 oz) fresh basil leaves,
  finely chopped
1 shallot, very finely chopped
1 tablespoon butter
300 ml ($\frac{1}{2}$ pint) fish or chicken
  stock
150 ml ($\frac{1}{4}$ pint) white wine

150 ml ($\frac{1}{4}$ pint) double cream
30 g (1 oz) freshly grated parmesan
  cheese
1–2 tablespoons olive oil
1 tablespoon pine nuts
2 small tomatoes, skinned, halved
  and insides scooped out
salt and freshly ground black
  pepper

Sweat half the basil and shallot in the butter until it softens slightly. Pour in the stock and reduce by half. Add the wine and reduce a bit further before adding the cream. Simmer until the sauce has a light coating consistency. Season with salt and pepper. Float a piece of cling-film over the top to stop a skin forming if the sauce is made in advance. Mash the remaining basil, shallot, pine nuts and olive oil together in a mortar and pestle. Add just enough parmesan to make a thick paste. Season with salt and pepper. Cover immediately to keep the green colour. The recipe can be done up to this point several hours ahead.

Paint the fish with olive oil and season. Grill for 3–4 minutes each side. Reheat the sauce. Stir half the pesto into the sauce and divide the remainder between the tomato halves. Serve the fish steaks with some sauce spooned over the top and decorated with a tomato cup.

Salad Niçoise with Fresh Tunny

Any number of different ingredients can be used for this classic salad, such as artichoke hearts, thin slivers of raw fennel, baby broad beans or indeed any of the baby vegetables now available.

serves 6

For the tunny
680 g (1½ lb) boneless fresh tunny
   steaks
3 tablespoons olive oil
several leaves fresh basil, shredded
1 tablespoon lemon juice

For the salad
230 g (8 oz) fresh small green beans
4 eggs, hard boiled, shelled and
   quartered
8 new potatoes, boiled and sliced
6 firm sun-ripened tomatoes,
   skinned and cut into wedges

8 anchovy fillets
small handful small black olives
½ a cucumber, peeled and sliced
4 spring onions, finely sliced
leaves from 3 different lettuces
½ cup of extra virgin olive oil
4 tablespoons wine vinegar
squeeze of lemon juice
some basil leaves, torn into
   small pieces
salt and pepper

Marinate the tunny steak in the olive oil, basil and lemon juice for a few hours if possible. Season them with salt and pepper. Heat a non-stick pan and cook the fish for about 3 minutes on each side. Remove the fish to a plate to cool, skin if necessary and divide into chunks.

Meanwhile blanch the beans in a large amount of boiling salted water until cooked *al dente*. Refresh under cold running water and drain.

Make the vinaigrette and use half to dress the lettuce. Arrange some leaves on 6 plates. Make individual piles of the other ingredients and arrange pieces of the tunny around the edge. Spoon some dressing over the beans and other ingredients but leave the tunny plain. Alternatively, you can mix the ingredients in a more casual way and set the tunny on top. Sprinkle some basil on the salads before serving.

Tunny Steaks with Onion Confit

If the tunny is very dark soak it in cold lightly salted water for 30 minutes. This dish can be served cold as well as hot.

serves 6

5 tablespoons of olive oil
680 g (1½ lb) onions, thinly sliced
70 g (2½ oz) caster sugar
5 tablespoons sherry vinegar
5 tablespoons red wine

6 170 g (6 oz) tunny steaks, skinned
seasoned flour
3 tablespoons groundnut oil
finely chopped fresh parsley
salt and pepper

Heat the olive oil in a large frying or sauté pan. Stir in the onions and some salt and pepper. Cover the pan and simmer gently for about 20 minutes. Add the sugar, vinegar and wine to the pan and continue to simmer for another 25 minutes, uncovered, or until the onions have absorbed the liquid and are very soft.

Dust the tunny steaks in the seasoned flour and sauté in the hot oil for a few minutes each side. Serve on a bed of the warm onions and decorate with a sprinkling of finely chopped parsley.

Grilled Tunny with Bouillabaisse Sauce

serves 4

580 g (1 lb 4 oz) boned fresh tunny,
cut 2 cm ($\frac{3}{4}$ inch) thick

For the marinade
2 tablespoons lemon juice
3 tablespoons olive oil
pinch of dried thyme
freshly ground black pepper

For the sauce
450 g (1 lb) mussels
300 ml ($\frac{1}{2}$ pint) dry white wine
3 shallots, finely chopped

2 garlic cloves, crushed
pinch of saffron
pinch each of dried thyme,
savory and oregano
several parsley stalks
1 medium tomato, skinned,
seeded and chopped
tiny pinch cayenne pepper
(optional)
80 g (3 oz) cold unsalted butter,
diced
salt and freshly ground black pepper
finely chopped parsley to decorate

Mix lemon juice, olive oil, thyme and some black pepper together; place the fish slices in a shallow dish and pour over the marinade. Cover and leave for 1–4 hours.

Wash the mussels in cold salted water, discarding any that are not tightly shut. Place them in a saucepan with 150 ml ($\frac{1}{4}$ pint) of the wine, the same of water, and 1 tablespoon of the shallots. Cover, bring to a boil, and continue boiling until mussels open, 3–5 minutes. Transfer mussels to a bowl with a slotted spoon. Strain mussel liquid through a muslin-lined sieve into a saucepan. Add remaining wine, shallots, garlic minus one sliver, saffron, dried herbs, cayenne pepper and parsley stalks. Simmer covered for 15 minutes, uncover, and reduce to about 5 tablespoons. Strain through a fine sieve pressing on the vegetables to extract all the flavour possible. Purée the tomato, and sliver of peeled garlic in a blender, slowly add the strained liquid. Return to a clean small saucepan. Don't worry if you find the taste fairly strong – it should be, and will change dramatically when the butter is added. The recipe can be prepared up to this point 8 hours ahead. Preheat the grill and cook the fish for 3–4 minutes each side. Remove to a heated dish. Reheat the sauce, whisk in the butter, on and off the heat, so the butter thickens the sauce and doesn't become so hot that it melts into it. Add the mussels and adjust the seasoning. Arrange the fish on 4 plates and spoon the sauce and mussels around the edge. Decorate with some finely chopped parsley.

Note: this sauce also goes well with other fish.

191

Tunny or Shark with Ginger
and Coriander Sauce

Well heated plates cook the thin slices of fish most effectively in this recipe adapted from Jeremiah Tower's *New American Classics*, (1986). With all the ingredients prepared and on hand, the recipe literally takes 5 minutes.

serves 4 as a first course

4 × 60 g (2 oz) 5 mm ($\frac{1}{4}$ inch) thick
   slices of tunny or shark
5 tablespoons butter
200 ml (good $\frac{1}{4}$ pint) fish stock
40 g ($1\frac{1}{2}$ oz) piece of fresh ginger,
   peeled and finely chopped

1 shallot, very finely chopped
3 tomatoes, skinned, seeded,
   and chopped
1 teaspoon, fresh coriander,
   chopped
salt and freshly ground black pepper

Place fish slices between cling-film and gently beat out until 3 mm ($\frac{1}{3}$ inch) thick. Spread 4 heat-resistant plates with $\frac{1}{2}$ teaspoons of butter each. Place in a hot oven or under a grill until hot. Remove the plates from the oven or grill, season the fish and place a slice on each plate. Mix the stock, ginger, shallots and tomato in a small sauté pan. Bring to the boil and cook 2 minutes, then whisk in the remaining butter. Flip the fish slices over, pour the sauce over the fish, garnish with the coriander and serve.

——— ••• ———

Stir-Fried Shark

serves 4

680 g (1½ lb) shark, cut into 2.5 cm
  (1 inch) pieces

For the marinade
3 tablespoons thin soy sauce
1 tablespoon medium-dry sherry
4 cm (1½ inch) peeled, chopped
  ginger
225 g (8 oz) oyster mushrooms
225 g (8 oz) mangetout, trimmed
  and blanched for 30 seconds

1 clove finely chopped garlic
2 shallots, finely chopped
1 tablespoon fresh finely chopped
  ginger
3 tomatoes, peeled, seeded and cut
  into strips
3 tablespoons groundnut oil
1 teaspoon cornflour
3 tablespoons chicken or fish stock
1 tablespoon oyster sauce

For the marinade; put half the chopped ginger in a garlic press with a few drops of water and squeeze the juice into a bowl. Discard the pulp and repeat with the remaining ginger. Add the soy sauce and sherry to the ginger juice. Turn the fish in the mixture and leave for 20 minutes.

Mix the cornflour with the cold stock and oyster sauce and set aside. Drain the fish. Heat 2 tablespoons of oil in a wok, add the fish and sauté lightly. Remove the fish with a spatula and set aside. Add the remaining oil to the wok and sauté the garlic, ginger and shallots for a few seconds. Add the mushrooms, salt and pepper and stir-fry until the mushrooms soften. Strain any fish juices into the cornflour mixture and add the fish to the wok. Stir for a few seconds, add the cornflour mixture, mangetout and tomatoes and bring to a boil. Serve immediately on warmed plates.

————— ••• —————

Swordfish or Shark with Aubergine Relish

The long thin variety of aubergine imported from Mediterranean countries is often a better bet than the hot-house Dutch variety. Walnuts too, need to be fresh so there is no hint of bitterness when eaten. Nuts of any variety should be stored in the freezer to stop deterioration.

serves 6

6 x 170 g (6 oz) swordfish,
  or shark steaks

For the marinade
1 small onion, finely chopped
1 tablespoon fresh parsley,
  finely chopped
1 bay leaf, chopped
2 tablespoons olive oil
squeeze of lemon juice

For the relish
450 g (1 lb) long thin aubergines
60 g (2 oz) shelled walnuts
4–5 tablespoons olive oil
pinch of allspice
pinch of cayenne pepper (optional)
salt and pepper
shredded lettuce to decorate
$1\frac{1}{2}$ tablespoon finely chopped
  coriander or mint

Marinate the fish for about 1 hour. Wipe dry, season, and cook for 4–5 minutes each side on a preheated grill.

    Meanwhile arrange the aubergines in a baking tin rubbed with olive oil, place in a moderate oven and bake until they are soft. When they are cool enough to handle cut them open and scoop out the insides. Place walnuts in a blender and purée, add the aubergine, olive oil and seasoning and blend until smooth. Before serving stir half the chosen herb into the purée and check seasoning. Serve the fish on individual plates decorated with a little shredded lettuce and a good dollop of aubergine relish sprinkled with the remaining chopped herb.

Variation: An alternative to the aubergine relish is *tapenade*, or olive paste (available at Italian grocers and some supermarkets). Spread a thin layer over the fish before serving.

Shark with Grilled Vegetables

This is a natural for barbeques but it can also be done successfully under a good grill.

serves 4

200 g (7 oz) shark, tunny or
  swordfish steaks
8 small leeks, well washed
4 small courgettes, cut lengthwise
  into quarters
2 red peppers

450 g (1 lb) firm small aubergines
olive oil
1 tablespoon fresh thyme, finely
  chopped
salt and pepper

Blanch the leeks in boiling salted water for 3 minutes, remove and set on tea cloths to drain. Add the courgettes to the pan, blanch for 2 minutes and drain. Place the peppers and aubergines in an oven dish, sprinkle with olive oil and season. Cover and set in an oven heated to 180°C/350°F/gas 4 for 20–25 minutes, or until tender. Remove the aubergines from the dish but leave the peppers, covered, until they cool down. Cut off the stems from the aubergines and slice lengthwise into quarters. Peel the peppers, discard seeds and core, and slice into thick strips. Carefully place all the vegetables in one layer in a dish and sprinkle with olive oil and half the herb. Sprinkle the fish with oil and the rest of the herb.

The vegetables can be grilled on the coolest part of the fire before you start the fish on the hotter part. Alternatively first grill the vegetables a lower distance from the heat source, remove and grill the fish quite close. Arrange a selection of vegetables with each fish steak and serve.

———— •●• ————

VEGETABLES

Vegetables

Grilled Polenta

Grilled polenta is good with all roasted or grilled game birds. It is also delicious fried in butter with a dryish game dish or used as a base for sitting small birds on.

300 g (10½ oz) coarse polenta-type
   cornmeal
1.7 litres (3 pints) water

Bring the water to a boil, add salt and pour in the polenta in a slow steady stream, stirring constantly with a wooden spoon. Keep stirring for about 30 minutes, until the polenta has an elastic texture and comes away from the sides of the pan. Spread out on a board or flat surface with a spatula to a thickness of about 2.5 cm (1 inch), leave to cool for at least 20 minutes. Cut into squares. Toast under a hot grill until light brown on both sides.

Game Chips

serves 6

600 g (1¼ lb) potatoes
groundnut oil for deep frying
salt

Peel and slice the potatoes as thin as possible. This can be done with a processor. Soak in cold water for 20 minutes then drain and dry, heat the oil until it reaches a temperature of 190°C/375°F. Fry a few at a time, shaking the basket so they don't stick together. Drain and salt lightly. Keep warm, uncovered, in a low oven. The coarse grating or julienne disc of a processor can make matchstick potatoes in the same way.

Celeriac Purée

serves 6

2 eating apples
1 potato
1 large celeriac

75 g (3 oz) butter
150–300 ml ($\frac{1}{4}$–$\frac{1}{2}$ pint) cream
salt and freshly ground pepper

Peel, core and slice the apples. Peel the potato and celeriac, and cut both into thick slices. Cook the apple, celeriac and potato in boiling salted water for about 20 minutes or until tender. Drain, then purée through a vegetable mill or potato ricer. Whisk in the butter and enough cream to make a light fluffy purée. Season with salt and pepper.

Note: To reheat, place in a bain-marie, stirring occasionally, until hot.

Potato Galette

These can be made in small individual sizes or in one large round. It is particularly nice to use as a base for small birds such as quail or partridge. It is fairly crucial to make it at the last minute.

serves 6

6 good-sized baking potatoes
45 g ($2\frac{1}{2}$ oz) clarified butter
salt and pepper

Peel the potatoes, dropping them into a bowl of cold water as you go. Dry them and grate on the coarse grater of a food processor or hand grater. Dry them in kitchen paper but do not put in cold water at this stage because the potatoes must retain their starch so they stick together in the pan. Cover the bottom of a 30 cm (12 inch) non-stick or heavy frying pan with a thin layer of clarified butter and heat until quite hot. Add the potatoes, sprinkle with salt and pepper and press down with a spatula to make an even layer. Shake the pan occasionally so they do not stick. When the bottom is nice and brown, in a few minutes, lower the heat and cook until the potatoes are tender, about 8 minutes. Keep an eye out that the bottom doesn't burn. Invert the galette on to a plate. Add more butter to the pan and slide the potatoes into the pan, brown side up. Raise the heat and cook just a few minutes to brown the under side. Serve as soon as possible.

Potato, Garlic and Rosemary Gratin

There are endless permutations of potato gratins and all of them go well with game. This particularly one uses no dairy products and can accompany grilled venison or pigeon breasts.

serves 8

5 tablespoons extra virgin olive oil
1.5 kg (3½ lbs) boiling potatoes
1 tablespoon fresh rosemary, finely chopped or ½ tablespoon of dried

7 cloves fresh garlic, peeled and thinly sliced
350 ml (good ½ pint) chicken stock
salt and freshly ground black pepper

Preheat the oven to 190°C/375°F/gas 5. Oil the bottom of a gratin dish. Peel and cut the potatoes into 3 mm (⅛ inch) thick. Layer about one-third of the potatoes in the dish. Season well with salt, pepper, half the rosemary, and half the garlic. Sprinkle with 1 tablespoon of olive oil. Make another layer using half the remaining potatoes, cover with the rest of the garlic, rosemary and some salt and pepper. Sprinkle with another tablespoon of olive oil. Cover with the rest of the potatoes, season, sprinkle with the olive oil and pour over the stock. Bake for about 1¼ hours, by this time the potatoes should be tender, the top crisp and brown and the stock absorbed.

Parsnip Chips

Use top 7.5 cm (3 inches) of the turnip (the rest can go for soup). Remove the hard core and slice thinly. Soak in cold water for 10 minutes, drain and dry well. Deep fry in small batches at 190°C/375°F until crisp. Drain, salt, and keep warm.

Parsnip French Fries

Use top third of parsnip only and cut into thin batons. Soak in cold water for 10 minutes. Deep fry until golden as above.

Celeriac Chips and French Fries

Celeriac can be used in the same way. Peel and slice thinly then soak in acidulated water for 10 minutes before draining, drying and frying.

Purée of Onions

serves 6

$\frac{3}{4}$ kg (1$\frac{1}{2}$ lb) sliced onions
4 tablespoons unsalted butter
150 g (5 oz) rice

$\frac{3}{4}$ litre (1$\frac{1}{4}$ pints) stock
2 tablespoons crème de cassis
salt and pepper

Blanch the sliced onions in a large quantity of boiling water for 3 minutes. Drain, then place in a heavy saucepan with half the butter. Stir for a few minutes to coat the onions in the fat then add the cassis. Stir in the rice then pour over the stock, add salt and pepper and bring to a boil. Reduce the heat and simmer gently, uncovered, until the rice is cooked. Purée in a processor or food mill. Reheat with the rest of the butter, season and serve.

Braised Onions and Rice

serves 6

120 g (4 oz) long-grain rice
900 g (2 lb) spanish onions, thinly
   sliced
85 g (3 oz) unsalted butter
4 tablespoons stock

salt and pepper
4 tablespoons cream
finely chopped parsley
salt and freshly ground black
   pepper

Blanch the rice in boiling salted water for 5 minutes then drain. Heat the butter in a 2½ quart flame-proof casserole. Stir in the onions, and continue to stir until the onions begin to wilt. Stir in the rice, the stock and some salt and pepper. Cover and place in an oven preheated to 150°C/300°F/gas 2 for about 1 hour. Stir the mixture half-way through the cooking time. Before serving stir in the butter, adjust the seasoning and garnish with the parsley.

Glazed Onions

serves 6

36 pickling onions, peeled
300 ml (½ pint) chicken stock
300 ml (½ pint) red wine

1 tablespoon sugar
30 g (1 oz) unsalted butter
salt and pepper

Place onions in a frying-pan large enough for them to fit in one layer. Pour over the stock, wine, sugar, half the butter, salt and pepper. Bring to the boil, then simmer, uncovered, until the onions are tender and all the liquid has evaporated. Add the rest of the butter, shake the pan to glaze the onions and serve.

——— ••• ———

Lentil Purée

serves 8

350 g (12 oz) brown lentils
1 onion, stuck with a clove
1 carrot, sliced
1 stalk of celery, sliced
bouquet garni

3–4 tablespoons good stock
60 g (2 oz) unsalted butter
salt and pepper
3 tablespoons of fresh coriander,
  finely chopped (optional)

Pick over the lentils and remove any grit. Combine the lentils with the vegetables, bouquet garni and 1.4 litres ($2\frac{1}{2}$ pints) of water in a saucepan. Bring to the boil, cover, and simmer until the lentils are tender, about 45 minutes. Add some salt for the last 10 minutes of the cooking time. Remove the onion and bouquet garni, then rub the lentils and vegetables through a sieve. Return to a clean pan and stir briskly over heat, add the stock and butter and season. Toss with the coriander just before serving.

Burghul with Herbs

serves 8

110 g (4 oz) each of finely chopped
  carrot, onion, and celery
4 tablespoons unsalted butter
2 tablespoons oil
450 g (1 lb) coarse burghul
small bunch of fresh parsley,
  finely chopped
1 tablespoon chopped fresh
  marjoram

1 teaspoon chopped fresh thyme
grated rind of one lemon
juice of $\frac{1}{2}$ lemon
60 g (2 oz) pine nuts
salt and freshly ground black
  pepper
3 tablespoons chopped fresh
  coriander leaves

Using a large frying pan, sauté the vegetables in half the butter until soft. Add the rest of the butter and the oil and stir in the burghul until well coated in the fat. Add half the parsley, all the marjoram and thyme and the lemon rind and juice. Pour in 1 litre ($1\frac{3}{4}$ pints) of water, season, and bring to the boil. Simmer, covered, very gently for about 25 minutes. The water should be absorbed and the grains separate. Turn into an oven dish, sprinkle with pine nuts and bake in a moderate oven 180°C/350°F/gas 4 for about 15 minutes. Stir in the coriander and remaining parsley and serve.

Swede with Apple

serves 6–8

1.25 kg (3 lbs) swedes	70 g (2½ oz) unsalted butter
3 Cox's orange pippins	4 tablespoons double cream
2 tablespoons lemon juice	gratings of fresh nutmeg
1 tablespoon sugar	salt and freshly ground black pepper

Peel and cut the swedes into equal-sized pieces. Boil in salted water to cover until tender. Drain well, purée, and mix in all but a knob of the butter, the cream, grated nutmeg, salt and pepper.

Peel, core and dice the apples. Place in a small saucepan with the knob of butter, sugar, lemon juice and 6 tablespoons of water. Cover and simmer over low heat until the apple is tender but still holds its shape. The recipe can be prepared in advance up to this point. Reheat the swede, stirring, over low heat. Add the apple, heat a few more minutes and serve.

Vegetable Purées

Vegetable purées go particularly well with game. They are also practical as they can be made in advance and reheated in a double saucepan or in the oven in buttered ramekins set in a bain-marie. The texture can be varied by using either a blender or food processor – the blender giving the finer texture. The purée should just fall from a spoon and it can be adjusted by thinning with cream or whisking over high heat to evaporate moisture and thicken. Leeks, artichokes, and fennel are some other vegetables that make excellent purées.

Parsnip Purée

serves 4-6

60 g (2 oz) unsalted butter
230 g (8 oz) onions, chopped
1 kg (2 lbs) parsnips, peeled and
   cut into chunks

300 ml ($\frac{1}{2}$ pint) chicken stock
6–8 tablespoons double cream
salt and pepper

Melt the butter in a large saucepan and gently soften the onions, then add the parsnips and stir to coat in the butter. Pour in the stock, cover, and simmer for 30 minutes or until parsnips are very tender. Turn into a blender and purée, return to the pan, season and stir in enough of the cream to make the desired consistency.

Brussel Sprout Purée

serves 4-6

1 kg (2 lbs) Brussels sprouts
60 g (2 oz) unsalted butter
150 g ($\frac{1}{4}$ pint) double cream

a few gratings of nutmeg
salt and pepper

Trim the stems and remove any discoloured outer leaves from the sprouts. Blanch them in a large quantity of boiling salted water for 2 minutes. Refresh under cold running water. Place the sprouts in steamer, cover, and steam until tender. Purée in a processor or blender with the butter. Turn into a saucepan, reheat, stirring, then season and add enough cream to make a purée that just falls from the spoon.

———— •●• ————

Carrot Purée

serves 4–6

1 kg (2 lbs) carrots, peeled and
   sliced
30 g (1 oz) unsalted butter

salt and pepper
a pinch of ground ginger
6–8 tablespoons double cream

Place the carrots in a saucepan with the butter and 150 ml ($\frac{1}{4}$ pint) of water. Cook over very low heat until the carrots are tender. Uncover and boil hard, shaking the pan occasionally, until the water has evaporated. Purée in a blender or processer. Season and reheat with the cream, stirring to evaporate any extra moisture.

Carrots and Parsnips with Rosemary

serves 8

10 carrots
8 parsnips
600 ml (1 pint) chicken stock
1 teaspoon fresh rosemary,
   finely chopped

45 g ($1\frac{1}{2}$ oz) unsalted butter, cubed
salt and freshly ground black
   pepper

Peel the carrots and parsnips and cut into 1 cm by 6.5 cm ($\frac{1}{2}$ in by $2\frac{1}{2}$ in)-sized batons. Bring the stock to a boil, add the carrots and simmer gently, covered until just tender. Remove with a slotted spoon, add the parsnips and simmer them in the same way until tender. Remove the parsnips and boil down any remaining stock to about 6 tablespoons. Swirl in the butter, return the vegetables and rosemary to the pan, season, mix together then serve.

——— •●• ———

Braised Celeriac

serves 4–6

1 large celeriac
250 ml (scant $\frac{1}{2}$ pint) good chicken
   stock

30 g (1 oz) unsalted butter
salt and pepper
finely chopped parsley to garnish

Peel the celeriac, cut into 1.3 cm ($\frac{1}{2}$ inch) slices, then cut the slices into 1.3 cm ($\frac{1}{2}$ inch) sticks. Simmer in the stock and butter with some salt and pepper, covered, for about 20 minutes or until tender. Uncover, boil hard to evaporate any remaining stock and serve sprinkled with parsley.

Braised Endive

Endive goes particularly well with game, braised as in this recipe or just sliced and stewed in a little butter or stock.

serves 6

12 firm tightly closed endive
   (witloof)
unsalted butter

juice of half an orange
2 tablespoon finely chopped
   parsley

Butter a flame-proof casserole large enough to hold the endive in two layers. Sprinkle with the orange juice, some salt and 6 tablespoons of water. Cover and simmer for 10 minutes. Uncover and boil until the liquid is reduced to about 3 tablespoons. Cover the endives with cartouche sheet of buttered paper and a lid. Bake in an oven pre-heated to 160°C/315°F/ gas $2\frac{1}{2}$ for 1 hour. Remove the lid but keep the paper in place and bake for a further 30 minutes.

—— ••• ——

Fried Parsley

This is one of the nicest accompaniments for fish and worth the trouble of deep frying.

2–3 sprays of curly parsley per person

oil for deep-frying
salt

Remove any tough parsley stalks. Wash well in cold water and spin dry, then pat dry with kitchen paper. Heat the oil to 185°C (360°F). Add the parsley, a handful at a time, and cook for about 45 seconds. Keep the parsley submerged with a slotted spoon if necessary. Drain on kitchen paper, sprinkle with salt and serve hot.

Parsley Purée

serves 6

350 g (12 oz) parsley leaves, (weighed after stalks have been removed)

110 ml (scant $\frac{1}{4}$ pint) double cream
a knob of unsalted butter
salt and freshly ground black pepper

Wash and drain the parsley. (This can be done most effectively in a salad spin-dryer.) Simmer in 450 ml ($\frac{3}{4}$ pint) boiling salted water for 10 minutes. Drain, then purée in a blender or food processor with the cream. Reheat with the butter and season.

Baked Grated Parsnips

serves 6–8

1.25 kg ($2\frac{1}{2}$ lbs) parsnips
60 g (2 oz) unsalted butter

salt and freshly ground black pepper

Peel then grate the parsnips. This can be done quickly in a food processor. Butter a baking dish and layer with grated parsnips, dotted butter, and salt and pepper. Bake in a moderate oven 180°C/350°F/gas 4 for about 45 minutes, cover the top with foil when it becomes brown, but allow it to form a crunchy top.

Potato and Celeriac Gratin

serves 6–8

900 g (2 lbs) potatoes, thinly sliced
1 large celeriac, peeled, quartered
    and thinly sliced

85 g (3 oz) unsalted butter
300 ml ($\frac{1}{2}$ pint) stock or light cream
salt and freshly ground black pepper

Butter a gratin dish and layer with the potatoes and celeriac. Season each layer with salt and pepper and dot with buter. End with a layer of potatoes dotted with butter. Pour over the stock or cream and bake in a moderate oven 180°C/350°F/gas 4 for about 1 hour. Cover the top if they brown too quickly. The celeriac goes a bit grey but it does not affect the excellent flavour.

Red Cabbage with Apples

serves 8

3 tablespoons unsalted butter
120 g (4 oz) piece of streaky bacon,
    cubed
1 medium-sized onion, chopped
medium head of red cabbage,
    cored and shredded

4 tablespoon wine vinegar
3 eating apples, peeled, cored and
    sliced
salt and pepper

Heat the butter in a large heavy saucepan, add the bacon and lightly brown. Add the onion and stir for a few minutes, then add the cabbage and stir until well coated in the fat. Mix in the vinegar and season with salt and pepper. Add the apples, cover, and simmer over very low heat (using a simmering disc if possible) for about 35 minutes, or until cabbage is tender but still has a bit of bite.

Variation: Add 240 g (8 oz) of peeled chestnuts to the cabbage. Dried chestnuts (about 140 g (5 oz)) can be used if first soaked in boiling water overnight.

SAUCES, COMPÔTES, STOCKS AND SOUPS

Sauces, Compôtes, Stocks and Soups

Quince Compôte with Cardamom

This is inspired by the excellent quince and cardamom compôte I tasted made by Franeis Bissell to accompany game pâtés. It could also be served with hot game pies or a joint of venison or boar.

makes 1 pint

230 g (8 oz) quince,
  (about 1 large one)
1 tablespoon lime juice

4 green cardamom pods, crushed
85 g (3 oz) sugar

Wash the quince well, quarter, core, cut into pieces and place in a saucepan. Add the lime juice and 150 ml ($\frac{1}{4}$ pint) of water. Enclose the cardamoms in a small muslin bag and add to the pan. Simmer, covered, until the quince is tender. Add the sugar and when it has dissolved, remove the cardamoms and pass the mixture through the fine disc of a food mill or sieve. Adjust the flavour by adding more sugar or lime juice as necessary.

——— ••• ———

Apricot and Clementine Sauce

Josceline Dimbleby's delicious invention that goes extremely well with game pâtés. It comes from *The Josceline Dimbleby Christmas Book*.

serves 4

230 g (8 oz) dried apricots
4 small clementines
1 medium-sized onion, peeled and
  roughly chopped

50 g (2 oz) soft brown sugar
1–2 tablespoons red wine vinegar
2–4 pinches cayenne pepper

Soak apricots in water for at least 2 hours. Cut unpeeled clementines into thin slices, discarding any pips. Put clementine slices, onion, cloves, sugar and drained apricots into a saucepan. Cover with water and bring to the boil. Reduce to a simmer, cover, and simmer very gently for 30 minutes, until soft and fairly thick. Stir vigorously to break up apricots. Add the vinegar and cayenne pepper to taste.

Spiced Damsons

1 kg (2 lb) damsons
1 kg (2 lb) sugar
150 ml ($\frac{1}{4}$ pint) cidrer or
  elderflower vinegar

4 blades of mace
1 stick cinnamon
1 teaspoon bruised allspice berries

Pierce the damsons with a needle. Place in a crock with all the other ingredients and leave for 2 days. Bring slowly to a simmer and simmer very slowly for 15 minutes. Seal while hot if you are planning to keep them any length of time, otherwise refrigerate and eat after 2 weeks.

—— •• ——

Spiced Kumquats

1 kg (2 lb) kumquats
1 kg (2 lb) sugar
1 stick cinnamon
$\frac{1}{4}$ teaspoon cloves

6 blades mace
4 cardamom pods
450 ml ($\frac{3}{4}$ pt) cider vinegar

Place the kumquats in a saucepan, barely cover with water and simmer, covered, for 10 minutes. Meanwhile, dissolve the sugar with the spices in the vinegar over gentle heat. Bring to the boil and boil for 5 minutes. Drain the kumquats and reserve the cooking liquid. Place the kumquats in the syrup and if necessary add some of the reserved liquid to just cover the fruit. Simmer very gently for 30 minutes. Remove from the heat and leave uncovered for 24 hours, turning the fruit in the syrup once or twice. Next day bring the kumquats and syrup back to the boil, drain the fruit and pack in sterilised jars. Bring the syrup back to the boil and boil hard to thicken slightly. Pour over the kumquats, distributing the spices between the jars and seal. Keep for 6 weeks before using.

Tomato and Tarragon Sauce

This is particularly nice for grilled or baked fish.

1 shallot, chopped fine
2 tablespoons extra virgin olive oil
2 cloves garlic, chopped very fine
2 teaspoons chopped tarragon

3 good pinches of sugar
300 ml ($\frac{1}{2}$ pint) chopped canned tomatoes
30 ml ($\frac{1}{2}$ pint) light fish stock

Gently soften the shallot in the oil then add the garlic, tomatoes, stock, sugar and some salt and pepper. Simmer uncovered until the quantity is reduced by about half. Sieve the mixture and return to the pan. Add the tarragon and simmer a few minutes more. Adjust the seasoning and serve.

—— ••• ——

Cold Tomato Sauce with Fromage Frais

Excellent with any cold fish dish and makes a change from the usual mayonnaise.

serves 4–6

625 g (1¼ lb) tomatoes, skinned, seeded and diced
6 tablespoons fromage frais
1 tablespoon chopped double cream

1 teaspoon chopped fresh tarragon
pinch of caster sugar
1 tablespoon tomato ketchup
2 teaspoons armagnac
salt and freshly ground black pepper

Lightly salt the diced tomatoes and place in a stainless-steel or plastic sieve to drain. Whisk the fromage frais with the cream then add the other ingredients. Fold in the tomatoes, taste for seasoning and refrigerate until needed.

Brown Chicken Stock

Makes about 600 ml (1 pint)

1.5 kg (3½ lbs) chicken wings or carcases, chopped
3 tablespoons oil
2 onions, chopped
2 carrots, chopped

1 stick celery, chopped
1 clove garlic, unpeeled
7 peppercorns, crushed
bouquet garni

Pour the oil into a large roasting pan and place in the top of a hot oven. When the oil is very hot add the chicken bones and wings, stir occasionally until they brown. Be careful not to char the bones or the resulting stock will be bitter. When the bones are nicely browned, add the vegetables, peppercorns and bouquet garni and continue to roast until the vegetables take on colour. Remove the pan from the oven and turn the contents into a large stockpot. Deglaze the roasting pan with water and add to the pot, add more water to the pot to cover the ingredients. Simmer the stock for one hour. Strain, then cool and refrigerate. Remove the surface fat when it has solidified. The stock can be further reduced depending on its taste and future use.

Note: The browning of bones and vegetables can also be done on top of the stove in a large sauté pan if more convenient.

Game Stock

Makes about 600 ml (1 pint)

1.5 kg (3½ lbs) chopped game
  bones and trimmings
4 tablespoons oil
2 onions, chopped
2 carrots, chopped
1 turnip, chopped

1 stick of celery, chopped
8 juniper berries
bouquet garni
300 ml (½ pint) white wine
salt and freshly ground black
  pepper

Roast the bones and trimmings with the oil in the top of a hot oven until brown. Stir occasionally and watch that the bones are not getting charred. Spoon off the oil, add the vegetables, juniper berries and bouquet garni and continue to roast for another 8 minutes or so to colour the vegetables. Remove from the oven and transfer to a large saucepan or stockpot. Add the white wine, a little salt and pepper and reduce by half. Cover the ingredients with water, bring to a boil, cover, and simmer for 1½ hours, skimming occasionally. Strain, then cool and refrigerate. Remove any surface fat when it has solidified. The stock can be further reduced depending on its taste and future use. The stock can be frozen.

Quail Consommé

serves 4

2 quails
1 tablespoon oil
1 carrot, chopped
1 stick of celery, chopped
2 shallots, unpeeled and quartered
bouquet garni

For the garnish
70 g (2½ oz) piece of celeriac
1 small carrot
2 tablespoons sherry or madeira
salt and freshly ground black pepper
finely chopped flat-leaved parsley

Remove the breasts from the quails and set aside. Heat the oil in a saucepan and brown the carcases and vegetables. Stir occasionally and take some time over this step so both vegetables and quail are well coloured but not burned. Add the bouquet garni and 1 litre (2 pints) of water. Bring to the boil, skim, and simmer for 45 minutes. Strain through a muslin lined sieve. Refrigerate when cool and leave for several hours. Skim off all the surface fat. Peel and cut both celeriac and carrot into thin batons of equal size. Simmer in a small amount of the consommé, lightly salted, until just tender, then drain. Just before serving, sauté the breasts in a non-stick pan for 2–3 minutes each side, cool, then slice into thin strips. Reheat the consommé, season, add the sherry, vegetables and quail slices and serve garnished with a tiny amount of very finely chopped parsley.

Fish Stock

Makes about 2 litres (3½ pints)

1 large onion, sliced
2 carrots, sliced
½ stalk of celery, sliced
white part of 1 leek, sliced
3 tablespoons olive oil

1.4 kg (3 lb) white fish bones and
   heads, gills removed
bouquet garni
300 ml (½ pint) white wine
8 peppercorns

In a large saucepan sauté the vegetables in the oil, stirring, for several minutes. Rinse the fish, add to the pan and stir a few more minutes. Add 3 litres (5 pints) of water and the bouquet garni. Salt lightly and bring to the boil. Skim when necessary and simmer for 15 minutes. Add the wine and peppercorns and simmer a further 15 minutes. Strain through a muslin-lined sieve. Cool, skim, then blot off any surface fat that remains.

Cream of Partridge Soup

Soup is an excellent way to use one old partridge. If you have a brace that are less than young remove the breasts for a quick sauté, following one of the pigeon breast recipes. The remaining legs and carcases will do for the soup.

serves 4

1 old partridge or 2 minus
   their breasts
1 onion, chopped
1 stick of celery, chopped
1 carrot, chopped
2 cloves garlic, peeled
bouquet garni
1 clove

300 ml ($\frac{1}{2}$ pint) dry white wine
1 shallot, chopped
225 g ($\frac{1}{2}$ lb) mushrooms
30 g (1 oz) unsalted butter
2 tablespoons flour
150 ml ($\frac{1}{4}$ pint) double cream
1 tablespoon madeira
salt and pepper

Heat a knob of butter in a saucepan, add the partridge, onion, celery, carrot, garlic, bouquet garni, and clove and stir for several minutes to coat the ingredients in the fat and slightly colour them. Add the wine and boil until it has evaporated. Cover with cold water, season with salt and pepper and simmer covered for $1\frac{1}{2}$ hours. Remove all the meat from the partridge and set aside. Discard the bones, bouquet garni and clove.

Saute the shallot in 1 tablespoon of butter, add the mushrooms, some salt and pepper and sauté until tender. Place the mushrooms, partridge meat and the pot vegetables in a processor with a ladle of the stock and purée.

Heat 30 g (1 oz) of butter in a saucepan, stir in the flour and cook for one minute. Pour in 750 ml ($1\frac{1}{4}$ pint) of the stock and whisk until smooth. Add the meat purée, bring to the boil and adjust seasoning and consistency, adding more stock if necessary. Stir in the cream and heat to just below the boil, add the madeira and serve.

———— ••• ————

Pheasant and Chestnut Soup

If you have used pheasant breasts for one meal the rest of the uncooked bird can be made into a delicious soup and pâté. The legs and thighs can be simmered in the stock until tender, the meat removed from the bone and blended with some butter to make a little pâté. The remaining stock forms the basis for the soup.

serves 4

carcases of 2 pheasants, chopped
2 tablespoons oil
1 onion, unpeeled and sliced
1 carrot, chopped
1 stick of celery, chopped
2 cloves garlic, crushed

bouquet garni, made with parsley
   stalks, bay leaf and sprig of thyme
glass of red or white wine
20 chestnuts, peeled
4 tablespoons double cream
salt and freshly ground black pepper

Heat the oil in a large heavy saucepan. Brown the carcases, pheasant joints, onion, carrot and celery over brisk heat, stirring occasionally. Add the garlic and bouquet garni. Pour in the wine and reduce by half. Add 2.75 litres (4 pints) of water, then simmer, covered, for 2 hours. If you are using the leg joints for pâté pull them out after 45 minutes. Strain the soup, refrigerate overnight when cool. Reheat the stock and reduce to 1.75 litres (3 pints). Chop the chestnuts coarsely and add to the soup. Simmer for 10 minutes, season and purée in a blender. Pour back into a clean saucepan, add the cream and serve.

Note: The juice of one orange, some gratings of orange rind and nutmeg can be used to make a variation.

———— •●• ————

Unusual Game

On 23 September, 1387, a royal feast was given to Richard II and the Duke of Lancaster by the Bishop of Durham. Among the birds and animals consumed were 12 boars, 3 tons of salt venison, 3 fresh doe, 50 swans, 400 large rabbits, 4 pheasants, 5 herons and bitterns, 100 dozen pigeons, 12 dozen partridges, 15 dozen curlews, 12 cranes and assorted wildfowl. . . .

In former centuries a far wider variety of animals, birds and fish were regularly consumed, some because they were (and some remain) edible and plentiful, others because they were, like the peacock or the swan, emblems of power and wealth, still others because they were all that could be found to fill the stomachs of the poor. Now we live in an overbuilt and overpopulated environment where many species which were killed for food, or their nests robbed of their eggs, are increasingly rare and often protected by law. It is still possible to come across unusual edible game, however, and this appendix lists a few kinds, and indicates briefly how they should be treated.

—— •●• ——

Birds

Wild Geese The season for the commoner species is the same as for wild duck and farmers may obtain an out-of-season permit if their crops are at risk. Wild geese are seldom found commercially, but if you are prepared to risk a fishy flavour and tough flesh, the older birds can be braised or stewed, and young birds roasted in the same way as domestic geese.

Black Game A relation of the grouse, this rare species is found in upland moors and forests. The male Blackcock and female Greyhen are only worth eating when young, and can be treated like grouse, though the flavour is less fine. Marinate in milk to remove the turpentiny flavour of pine needless.

221

Capercaillie Larger than their relations the grouse and black game, they need thorough hanging and long roasting.

Ptarmigan Creatures of the 'high tops' where their white winter plumage camouflages them from predators. They can be tough and junipery, but can also be delicious roasted and served with a sharp sauce.

Moorhen These common birds are seldom eaten, but skinned and browned in fat, the breasts and legs can make a good salmis or braise.

Rook Rook Pie is the best known way to cook these gregarious and voracious birds, and was popular in country districts and during the Second World War. Dorothy Hartley, in *Food in England* (1954), recommends simmering the skinned breasts in milk and water till tender, then buttering a deep pie dish and placing in it a juicy slice of raw beef with the cooked breasts in an overlapping layer over the meat. Thin strips of bacon are strewn over the breasts, the dish covered with a crust and the pie baked briskly before serving hot with a mustard sauce. They are notorious carriers of parasites.

Starling Another bird which is sometimes shot to protect crops. If you have a great many, they can be lavishly buttered, seasoned with juniper and pot-roasted.

Swan In Britain, wild swans on the Thames belong either to the Crown or to two of the City Livery Companies and are protected. If young, they can be roasted in a flour and water crust and served like a goose, carefully seasoned. If older, they must be stewed and are hardly worth eating.

Peacock Its plumage made this handsome bird the centrepiece for grand banquets in the past, but it is not now thought worth the trouble, being stringy and dry.

Smaller birds Song birds – thrushes, blackbirds and larks, for example—were much eaten in the past, and until recently in Europe, in pies, pâtés and skewered for the grill, but are now mainly protected by law.

Wild birds' eggs Eggs and nests are now protected by law, though landowners may obtain a special licence to collect and sell gulls' and plover's eggs. Quails' eggs are invariably farmed.

Animals

Squirrel Red squirrels, now confined to a few areas of the British Isles, are protected. Grey squirrels are classed as vermin because of the damage they do to trees and other wildlife. They need careful marinating before casseroling with vegetables.

Hedgehog Traditionally a Romany dish, covered in wet clay and baked in the embers, the hedgehog is said to be a delicacy reminiscent of suckling pig. A more modern method is to skin and split it before seasoning and grilling.

Badger Another protected species, except where culling is officially carried out. In the past, and for the occasional traffic victim in country areas today, the fat autumn badger makes two excellent smoked and salted hams.

Guinea Pig Not a native, and hardly a game animal, but one which has become a useful source of protein, roasted or jointed and fried, especially among town-dwellers in South America, where one mature animal will feed an adult.

Dormouse Large edible dormice were released at Tring Park in 1902 by Lord Rothschild, and the Romans regarded them as a great delicacy, fattening them in special earthenware pots (hence perhaps the treatment of the Dormouse at the Mad Hatter's Tea-party). They should be stuffed with a strong pork forcemeat and baked. The small native dormouse of the cornfields is uncommon and protected by law.

Snakes Only the grass snake can be eaten. Stewed, it resembles unfishy but equally bony eel.

Bibliography

Beedell, Suzanne, *The Compleat Angler's Wife*, 1964
Bery, Odette J., *Another Season Cookbook*, 1986
Borton, Paula, *The Great Game Book*, 1986
David, Elizabeth, *French Provincial Cooking*, 1960
De Salis, Mrs, *Dressed Game and Poultry A la Mode*, 1888
Dimbleby, Josceline, *The Josceline Dimbleby Christmas Book*, 1987
Drysdale, Julia, *Classic Game Cookery*, 1975
Ellis, Eleanor A., *Northern Cookbook*, 1967
Fletcher, Nichola, *Game For All*, 1987
Fitzgibbon, Theodora, *The Art of British Cookery*, 1965
Fitzgibbon, Theodora, *Game Cooking*, 1963
Game, 'The Good Cook' series, Time-Life Books 1982
Green, Henrietta, *British Food Finds*, 1987
Grigson, Jane, *English Food*, 1974
Grigson, Jane, *Jane Grigson's Vegetable Book*, 1978
Howard, Lady Constance, *Everybody's Dinner Book* 1890
McNeill, F. Marian, *The Scots Kitchen* 1929
Pollard, Major B. C., *The Sportsman's Cookery Book*, 1926
Schwabe, Calvin W., *Unmentionable Cuisine*
Stobart, Tom, *The Cook's Encyclopaedia*
Tower, Jeremiah, *New American Classics*, 1986
Wolfert, Paula, *The Cooking of South-West France*, 1983

Index